MARTIN WILSON

THE LITTLE BOOK OF

ANGER

Matador
9 Priory Business Park,
Wistow Road, Kibworth Beauchamp,
Leicestershire. LE8 0RX
Tel: (+44) 116 279 2299
Fax: (+44) 116 279 2277
Email: books@troubador.co.uk
Web: www.troubador.co.uk/matador

ISBN 978 1780882 208

British Library Cataloguing in Publication Data.
A catalogue record for this book is available from the British Library.

Typeset in 11pt Adobe Garamond Pro by Troubador Publishing Ltd, Leicester, UK
Printed and bound in Great Britain by TJ International Ltd, Padstow, Cornwall

Matador is an imprint of Troubador Publishing Ltd

For Julia

'*Anger makes dull men witty, but it keeps them poor.*'
– Francis Bacon

THE LITTLE BOOK OF ANGER

As you get older, that is, beyond the age of about eight, the irritation gene begins to develop. Perpetual sunshine and green grass and smiley rabbits no longer complete your world and, almost imperceptibly, you realise that some things are not perfect. What starts as a nebulous questioning of what goes on around you develops, with increasing maturity, into a critical faculty which has, at its extremes, a spirit of enquiry on the one hand, and intemperate cynicism on the other. That being so, it is difficult to understand why there are so many, generally small, books available (notably at airport bookshops) of the "Little Book of Happiness" genre.

This is intended to be an antidote. I suppose that a major cause of irritation to some people are those who cannot restrain themselves from offering their opinions on every subject and upon which they are unassailed by any doubt that they might, possibly, be wrong about anything. Conscious of that, I nevertheless tender my contribution: this is my Little Book of Things That Annoy Me.

TELEVISION JOURNALISTS

What is it about them that make them so irritating? Well, I suppose the most obvious thing is their hand-waving. They do not seem capable of saying anything without exaggerated gesticulation. Just watch the next time you turn on the news and see a reporter explaining some perfectly simple concept with the aid of sweeping gestures and bouncing hands. And why do they say "absolutely" as soon as they have been introduced and have taken over the item? Absolutely what? If the implication is supposed to be that the journalist's enthusiasm is boundless, does that mean that a lesser colleague should start by saying "Partially"? It is a particularly meaningless word to use when it normally follows an anodyne question from the anchor, such as "Jim, you are outside Scotland Yard now?" "Yes, absolutely."

But, given that the reporter is standing outside Scotland Yard, near that faintly ridiculous but much photographed revolving sign, the next question is: why are you standing there? The topic under discussion may concern a wide range of police-related topics but it is difficult (no, let's be frank, it's impossible) to see how the reporter's being outside the building is going to enlighten the viewer or facilitate comprehension. The poor journalist (and here a touch of sympathy creeps in, reluctantly) has driven from a comfortable studio or even his or her home, taking with him a cameraman and a sound recordist, possibly in dreadful weather, possibly through London's slow traffic so that he can stand outside the building and tell his tale. Assuming that there are archive photographs of most public buildings and assuming further (and this is not an immediately obvious assumption to make) that there is some dramatic enhancement in having the building as the background, I fail to see why he has to traipse over to SW1. It cannot, surely, be that they expect something momentous or even moderately newsworthy to happen: a deputy assistant commissioner throwing himself from the top of the building, for instance, or a cabinet minister being bundled into the back of a police car with an officer's hand on the top of his head in the manner of a crime drama. No, it is, plainly, because some dunderhead long ago decided that to be outside the building would, in some undefined way, add verisimilitude to the story and, with a complete lack of independent thought, it caught on and now this is how it is always done. That there is no other explanation is illustrated by the following. There are often noteworthy criminal trials that catch the public's attention and take place outside London. The jury returns its verdict at, say, 3.00 pm and, if there has been a conviction, the judge adjourns the case for sentence until, say, the following day or until pre-sentence or psychiatric reports are available. So the defendant is driven off to prison and the jury, the judge, the barristers and solicitors, the police officers, the families of the victim and of the prisoner, in fact, everyone, goes home. The cleaners come in and start work. It is now 7.00 pm and, live on the early evening news, a television journalist is outside the Crown Court, in the pouring rain, in the dark, with a piece on the trial and the verdict. Is it believed that the item will be given more impact if it comes from outside the court? Presumably so, and most probably that is because the journalist thinks (no, that is too strong an assumption because it is hard to divine what process of logic would arrive at this conclusion; it is more likely that he feels) that there is more credibility in a report that comes from outside the arena than from inside a studio.

That is not, of course, limited to court reporting; we have all seen zoom-in pictures of the exterior of hospitals, for instance, where an outbreak of MRSA or an unfortunate mix-up of blood samples has occurred. That is the subject of the report and we are supposed to be able to absorb it better if we are shown the sign for the outpatients' department in close-up.

Misuse of English is another serious fault of many television journalists, but it is not limited to them and is so widespread that it merits a section of its own. Nevertheless, I am conscious that some of the crassness of their reports may not be wholly, or at all, their fault. It may well be down to production and post-production.

PRODUCTION AND POST-PRODUCTION

Presumably the same pseudo-thought process is employed when we are shown wholly uninformative photographs or video footage as the background to a report. Some slightly post-adolescent studio director must once have decided that, when a news item relating to finance was reported, we should be shown pictures of bank notes and pound coins and that, if it concerned mortgage interest rates, it should be of a row of houses, some with 'For Sale' boards up. When there was controversy over the sale of Cadbury to an American conglomerate, we were helped to understand the social and fiscal complexities by being shown pictures of bars of chocolate. If the topic is children, we see feet in a school playground. We, of course, never see the children's faces because of some strained misunderstanding of the law: for Heaven's sake, we can see children if we look out of the window, that doesn't make us paedophiles or invaders of their privacy; but we do see their feet, lots of them, just as we are shown footage of lots of people (for some reason, usually crossing what looks like Waterloo Bridge) when the item concerns, in some way, the population in general or sections of the population. I once saw the same shot used when the topic was obesity. These pictures add nothing to the story other than to make me shout at my wife, poor darling, "So, that's what money looks like!" or "Haven't those children got a lot of feet!"[1]

There must be a pecking order in broadcasting. You start as a radio producer with the BBC and think it a good idea to have supposedly apt music to accompany serious news commentary. Thus, to go with an, admittedly, rather dull piece on secondary school class sizes, you insert as an introduction, a few bars from 'I Don't Need No Education' and, rather than getting demoted for that inanity, you either do it again or find the idea taken up (for, yes, I have heard it done three times) and find yourself promoted to a television production manager where you believe that you are the first person to conceive of the idea of having someone interviewed at the wheel of his car – and not just at the wheel, but actually driving. This is for no discernible purpose – the interviewee is not talking about driving or anything even marginally connected with road transport – but he turns towards the cameraman who is, presumably, squeezed uncomfortably with his equipment in the front passenger seat and puts everyone's life at risk as he gives his views on welfare reform or the burgeoning of Starbucks. Then, having established himself as a someone who can reuse hackneyed situations, the young director goes on to post-production and gives us pictures of houses and feet.

---

[1] On the evening before I wrote this, the BBC News on television announced that the National Union of Railwaymen had voted, by a small majority, in favour of strike action. The item was accompanied by a picture of a train.

After a period doing that, he is promoted to documentaries. Of course, I am guessing at this, just as my conjecture is that the thought of better pay may lure him to one of the commercial stations. He is, after all, nearly nineteen years old and has to think of his future. So there he is, with a script in front of him. A historian (of whom a small but serious gripe comes later on) has written something on, say, the Wars of the Roses. It is very well written (apart from the grip – just be patient) and the historian, who will present the piece himself, is photogenic and lucid and can be relied upon to keep the audience interested. The problem is that there is an hour-long slot allowed for it and, even with a modest speed of delivery, it is unlikely to last more than forty minutes. So, the producer falls back on post-production dramatic re-enactments. The result is that, at every mention by the historian of the word 'battle' there is a shot of actors dressed in mediaeval costumes, bashing each other with swords and clubs and at every mention of 'murder' we see a dank passageway in a castle and a couple of figures, barely discernible in the darkness; but, as this footage is, itself, only a few minutes long, we see the same thing over and over again and, with commercial television, at the tedious recapitulation at the end of every advertising break. Thus, by an alchemy almost worthy of the mediaeval period itself, these fools transform the highly watchable into the unbearable.

Generally speaking, though, radio journalism and radio production with (or perhaps, because of), the restricted possibilities for interference are of a much higher standard than on television. Not always so with newspapers journalists.

THE PRESENT HISTORIC

With one or two notable and eloquent exceptions, it has become *de rigeur* for historians, on the radio, on television and, I suspect, when lecturing students, to behave as if the past did not exist and that every event in human life is occurring now, as we speak. Just you listen, the next time that one of them broadcasts. The past tense of any verb is obliterated and, instead, we have the constant use of the present historic. It cannot be denied that it can be a very effective tool and may add a dramatic frisson to a story but, surely, in small doses and occasionally and only when called for. Instead we are bombarded with it: "Charles the First lives from 1600 until he is executed in 1649"; "Gladstone holds the office of Prime Minister which he alternates with Disraeli"; "War is declared when Germany invades Poland"; and "As a result of the Geneva Accords, Ho Chi Minh is now President of North Vietnam". Really? I thought that they were all dead.

Please, please you learned academics; give the present historic a rest. Save it for when you think that you really need it and, even then, ask yourselves whether it is truly necessary. It really is very annoying, you know and, at worst, can be misleading when your listeners (that is to say, I) don't know whether you are talking about something which happened in the past or is the current state of affairs.

PRINT JOURNALISTS AND THE
ATTEMPTED MURDER OF ENGLISH

The serious problem with print journalists is that they are, so often, completely wrong. They either fail to check their facts or make things up in the mistaken belief that their readers would not know, one way or the other, whether what they are reading is accurate. This implies either carelessness or arrogance; I suspect that, more often than not, it is both. Anyone who has any expertise in a particular field will have recoiled at serious misrepresentations perpetrated in newspapers, often by journalists who are supposedly specialist correspondents. I happen to know a bit (well, more than the average layman) about the law. Section 43(3) Criminal Justice Act 2003 empowers a judge of the Crown Court, in certain circumstances, to order that a *trial on indictment* may be conducted without a jury. That power was exercised for the first time, and upheld by the Court of Appeal, recently. The legal correspondent of a serious newspaper reported the decision as meaning that, for the first time for nearly four hundred years, a criminal trial would be held in England without a jury. Well, what did the reporter think that benches of three lay magistrates and solitary district judges (formerly called stipendiary magistrates) have been doing, week in, week out for years and years? The same correspondent (whose blushes I will spare by not identifying) once demonstrated ignorance of the difference between conviction and sentence.

But it is not limited to what some might see as no more than technical errors in specialised subjects. Basic mistakes abound – towns put in the wrong county, guesses turned into asseverations, a journalist's opinions given the cloak of authority by phrases such as "according to sources", "experts believe" or "it is estimated that". At the conclusion of every major criminal trial, when the verdict has just been delivered and even before sentence has been passed, there is almost always the information that the costs of the trial are estimated at some eye-watering figure. But estimated by whom? Certainly not by the lawyers involved or by the court officials because this is a long and complex process and sometimes takes weeks to resolve. So the estimate must be the reporter's based upon no foundation whatsoever.

My other main gripe with print journalists is that they so often misuse our beautiful and practical English language. I know, I know that language grows organically, that it is improved by the importation of new words, that William Shakespeare created myriad words that have since become part of common and accepted usage and, of course, that is all true. But is does not excuse the misuse of existing words so as to imply an entirely different and erroneous meaning; if it did, what would be the purpose of words having a meaning if they could be used to mean anything the writer chooses? Naturally, I am aware that the fault does not lie just with journalists, for politicians and pundits and radio presenters and sports commentators and lawyers are also guilty. But language is the tool of journalists and, unlike the speaker of words, the writer of words has the chance to consider and measure what he says. So when they use the word 'forensic' when they mean 'scientific', or 'epicentre' when they mean 'centre', or 'parameter' when they mean 'perimeter', or 'spiralling' when they mean 'increasing', or 'issue' when they mean 'problem', or 'incredibly' when they mean 'very', well, I groan. And when did they decide that an avatar was, in fact, an animated cartoon character? Or that a religious painting (an icon), whose name was used in the early days of computer language to mean a graphic symbol should, as an adjective, mean something akin to heroic or significant? And even when using the meaning of words accurately, the temptation towards the trite and, therefore, in effect, the meaningless seems beyond their powers of resistance. Thus, the term 'award-winning'. Hardly any playwright's name appears in a theatre criticism with that prefix, but I have seen it attached to the word 'mortgage'. What award? Who gave it? And why?

THE ASSAULT ON ENGLISH

I have already referred to the way in which words are misused. In some cases, the fault lies simply in hackneyed usage. So when, in 1986, the Challenger Space Shuttle blew up it executed a ghastly helix and it really did spiral out of control (no carping here that 'spiral' is being used as a verb). But now nothing goes out of control other than in a spiral; and what has become particularly strange and, at least to me, very irritating, is that solecism has been grown from cliché so that the word has come be used to mean 'increase'. So we learn, for instance, that the projected cost of the Olympic Games is spiralling. But it isn't – it is increasing, steadily and in a depressingly straight line. And, cliché upon cliché, there is usually one or two adverbs attached, so that a debt spirals upwards or assets spiral downwards. Why does nothing spiral forwards or backwards? Probably because the user does not think that simple and clear words like 'increase' or 'decrease' will do.

And, in case you couldn't be bothered to look them up, 'forensic' means relating to law courts, 'epicentre' means over or close to the centre (as distinct from the centre itself) and 'parameter' means, well, something so technical that only a mathematician can understand it, but two of them cannot have anything between them, so "within these parameters" is, decidedly, nonsense.

Another word that has been so frequently misused that its real meaning has been overwhelmed by its recent treatment is 'louche'. It's a French word that means shifty or dubious, and that is the sense that it has always been used in English. It also, in French, means a ladle and, sometimes, a handshake. But some fashion–leading dunderhead decided to use it as a term of mischievous approbation; as an adjective to describe a roguish, always male, sexual scallywag. I wonder how many actors, glowing with barely suppressed conceit at seeing themselves described as 'louche' appreciate that, in reality, they are being called dishonest, or a kitchen implement.

'Iconic', again, for it is another one. An icon is a representation of someone sacred, normally in the form of a painting or sculpture. It is not the personage him or herself. That is why 'iconoclasm' refers to the destruction of *images*. By repeated misuse 'iconic' is now employed to mean something like 'important' or 'acclaimed' and is applied to everything from buildings to scenery to pop singers. I do not object to the use of the word 'icon' in the computer sense, for it has a specialised and reasonably accurate meaning in that context. But, please, not Elton John.

And talking of gods, an *avatar* is a Hindu deity who, according to legend, descended to this world in the form of a human or animal. It is a Sanskrit word, so Hindus ought to know. But they may now be wrong, because Hollywood and the software industry have, in the last few years, taken to using the word as if it meant some sort of cartoon character and where those two behemoths lead the rest of us must eventually follow and so, in this instance too, we are in the inexorable process of the destruction of a rather beautiful word.

This does, of course, sound like the carping of an old crap. Of course, to some extent it is; but just because you get angered by ill-treatment of language does not axiomatically mean that you are wrong to do so. I have read Noam Chomsky and Steven Pinker and Guy Deutscher and have a pretty strong hold on the concept that language develops and words may change their meanings over time, and I can think of words that have even come to mean the opposite of what they originally conveyed, such as 'splice', 'cleave', 'let' and 'overlook' and others which have swapped their meanings with each other, such as 'clown' and 'fool', and 'curate' and 'vicar'. Nevertheless, words are the main tools by which we communicate thoughts and it seems to me that there is a strong case for objecting when a word which has a perfectly good and clear meaning is erroneously employed to indicate something wholly different and for doing so before the rot sets in and it loses its meaning altogether. I'll give you a good example. There is a wonderfully potent word that used to mean wickedness that was so great that it was monstrous. Even now, it has a ring to it that causes a frisson when attached to the description of some terrible crime: that word is 'enormity'. It had nothing to do with size, but some time ago it began, wrongly, to be used to mean 'very bigness', and now even a science journalist at 'The Times' talked of '...the sheer enormity of the solar system', and presumably did so because it sounds like 'enormousness' which is the sense that he intended to convey. Even the thesaurus on the computer programme with which I am writing this now gives that as a secondary meaning, but it is still wrong. We are witnessing the loss, through misuse, of a powerful word and by the same process as that by which we will lose 'niggardly' because some self-appointed, American college campus-based arbiters of what is acceptable (shades of 'The Human Stain'), think that it sounds like something else.

As for 'incredible' doesn't it mean 'not capable of belief', just as credible means the opposite? So when a judge says that he finds a witness's testimony credible, he does not mean that he thinks that it doesn't amount to much. But incredible is constantly used as meaning a great deal and incredibly as if it mean 'very', so the antonyms should mean the reverse. Of course 'credible' still has its proper meaning and some people continue to use 'incredible' or its adverb accurately but as, more often than not, 'incredibly' is used, including by prime ministers, in place of the simple word 'very', it was not surprising to hear a cotton-wool brained (but very pretty) actress, in interview, describe her role as 'incredibly believable'. And how about this? On the BBC no less, a televised dramatisation of an incident at sea during the Second World War was introduced as 'an incredible, true story' and the advertisements for serious films employ the same contradiction. But I suppose that the word has been used so often in this inappropriate way that it is now part of accepted usage, just as 'terribly' became a synonym for very. Perhaps it is beginning to replace it; and it will be incredibly difficult to stop it. Don't you believe it.

There is something that we all can recognise, because its misuse is so recent that the word is still, mostly, used in its proper sense. The old French *garderobe* gave rise to the modern English 'wardrobe' in a way that is simple to see; indeed, the words 'ward', 'warden' and 'warder' still maintain the sense of keeping someone or something protected. So the word wardrobe conjures up a either a solid piece of furniture which takes up a lot of space in the bedroom or, more frequently nowadays, a space with shelves, a hanging rail and doors fitted into the room: its purpose is to keep clothes in. Fashion journalists have decided, though, that the word should be used to mean, not the cupboard, but its contents, thereby demonstrating an inability to understand what must be one of the clearest derivations of a word. Consequently, we have the entertaining image thrust on us of a young starlet staggering along in her killer heels and fashionable clothes under the weight of a huge piece of furniture because, we read, she always travels with a large wardrobe.

Another example of a word that has, in the last few years, become part of accepted parlance through constant misuse is 'issue'. It used to have four distinct meanings: children, particularly in the upper-class context of 'he died without issue', an edition of a publication such as a book or magazine, a verb meaning to come forth (to which the first two meanings are linked) and the defined point of an argument or disagreement, as in 'the issue between the parties relates to damages and not to liability'. Somehow or other, it started to be used by cheesegrater voiced actresses who sought to sound intelligent, as if it meant 'problem'. Who can forget the initial astonishment on hearing that a person with some sort of perceived psychological deficit was described as 'having issues'? Evidently, the answer is, most people, as the next stage was to say 'I have an issue with that' meaning either (a) 'I don't like it, or (b) 'I don't understand it (but nor do I want you to think me an idiot)'. So now, on almost any web-based help site you see, not answers to questions or problems, but answers to issues. A short time ago I heard someone say that he had an issue with a restaurant by which, almost certainly, he meant that he did not like the food; and so, in a very short space of time, we see a word being used for the wrong meaning when there are other perfectly good words available simply and efficiently to convey the thoughts of the speaker or writer.

Talking of a short time, why do television announcers say that something will happen in "an hour's time"? What's wrong with 'in an hour'? What else could it be: an hour's length or weight? How about smell? I rather like that: "This programme was due to be shown in fifteen minutes' aroma but, due to technical difficulties, it will now be shown in two hours' stench."

Finally, and loosely, in this area is the, not so much misuse, as overuse of the word 'head'. You look surprised – you haven't noticed that it is overcooked, and can't see what is wrong with its use. Well, now that I have brought it to your attention, just look out for the numbers of times that you see the terms 'head out (or off) to' when 'go' would be sufficient and appropriate. I recently read a novel by a successful writer, who had his characters heading off to the garden or out of the house on almost every other page. And haven't you noticed 'head-to-head'? Of course you have, since I mention it. No-one ever seems to confront or compete with anyone these days: they go head-to-head.

WINE SNOBBERY

The English-speaking countries are, as far as I know, unique in maintaining the concept that there is some sort of moral elevation in possessing a highly-refined palate. I speak with the authority of someone who is bereft of that quality – I very much enjoy drinking wine, but cannot begin to distinguish between growths and vineyards and, evidently, more shame-worthy, cannot justify the difference between, say, a £15 and a £30 bottle. That is not to say that there is no difference or that there are not people who can discriminate between them, it is simply that I and, I suspect, the majority of those who claim to be able to, cannot do it, and so the question arises: why in some circles is it regarded as some sort of moral turpitude akin to incest not to have that facility? It is, after all, a physical attribute; no-one thinks the worse of another because he is short-sighted or has less than acute hearing, and whilst the ability to run fast or kick a ball accurately is admired (at least, in some circles), I have not encountered that slightly raised eyebrow and curled upper lip, directed at the less than athletic, that a display of oenological insensitivity can generate.

And what about descriptions? In my simplicity, I expect bread to taste of, well, bread. I would not be altogether happy if my jar of breakfast marmalade tasted of something other than orange jam. When it comes to wine, however, it is not good enough that it tastes of wine or anything like the product of fermented grape juice. All sorts of olfactory comparisons have to be drawn by wine writers. I suppose that flavour is a difficult thing to describe and there is a case, just, for pointing out that a New Zealand Sauvignon Blanc can remind you of the taste of gooseberries and that a French Chardonnay may have a *soupçon* of vanilla. But descriptions have lost all touch with reality. I once copied what was written on the label on the back of a bottle of Merlot from the Hunter Valley. It described the wine as having 'forest floor notes with varietal mint'. If any Australian, casually drinking in the forest, had so much that he fell to the ground and swallowed a mouthful, I doubt that he would have remembered what it tasted like when he sobered up but, if not him, then can it be that, on the route to becoming an Ozzie master of wine, you are obliged to eat what you are standing on? If so, the possibilities are too dreadful to contemplate; so let us pass on to the mint. In my ignorance, I had not hitherto appreciated that wine was supposed to taste of mint and I am not sure that, if I had, I would have bought that wine which was, as it happens, very good and tasted, to me, of wine; but what are we to make of 'varietal'? I simply do not understand what that is mean to suggest, because every mint is, presumably, an example of its own variety.

There is a tragedy in all this: these absurd descriptions are now beginning to appear on bottles of malt whisky.

BASEBALL CAPS

I have, actually, nothing against baseball caps. They look quite good on baseball players, and as a fashion statement for twenty-year-olds and younger they are reasonably acceptable. Their large peaks also provide a decent amount of shade and you can see the purpose of them when the tropical sun burns and blinds. In all other circumstances, it should be an indictable offence to wear them; I would be prepared to support the reintroduction of corporal punishment if it would go any way towards preventing middle-aged men from trying to look trendy by sporting them. What possible reason can there be for wearing them in cars or on trains or aeroplanes? Wearing them backwards by anyone above the age of fifteen merits racking, or, at least, branding with a hot iron. Institutionalised baseball caps by, for example, police forces are appalling – what possible use are they? Why the change from existing practical uniform headwear?

The justification that they provide protection from the sun is completely negated when sportsmen are being interviewed in a television studio after the match. Nevertheless, there is something which compels almost all cricketers and tennis players to sit there, giving largely inane answers to stupid, anodyne questions, with a baseball cap wedged firmly over the brow. Two questions always rise to the surface of my mind: Why are you sitting indoors with your hat on? and Why weren't you wearing it when you were out there playing?

Racing drivers wear very sensible headgear as they hurl their cars around the track; their helmets are, plainly, intended to protect them from serious injury and they can now incorporate all sorts of technical gadgetry which helps increase performance and, probably, marketing potential, but as soon as the race is over and they get out, the first thing they do is put on baseball caps. They all do it. You never see them without them. Then they compound this regimented idiocy by shaking up Jeroboams or Rehoboams of champagne which it has taken honest winemakers years to produce, and spraying the contents, like suicidal machine-gunners, over themselves and anyone standing within range.

This may all sound directed against men and, mostly, it is, but there is another, distinctly female, type of irritating baseball cap wearer and that is the footballer's wife with her designer jeans, her literally staggering heels, her enormous dark glasses meant to disguise her 'celebrity' (and, of course, having the opposite effect), and her ponytail sticking through the space between the back of the hat and the strap. Is that the only hat you can find, dear? What a shame. On the other hand, an attractive young woman, on a beach, well, maybe there is some point to them... No, I will not weaken.

AND T-SHIRTS

The T-shirt is another item of clothing which starts its existence in a perfectly anodyne way but may be turned into something which generates a range of reactions, from the smirk to the guffaw and, on the way, passes through irritation to something stronger than that; probably contempt.

The smirk comes from the way, and by whom, it is worn. Men who are unaware of the profile of their bodyline tend to favour T-shirts on hot days, perhaps thinking that they look like the cowboy in the old Marlboro cigarette advertisements when, in fact, they are projecting nothing other than their stomachs, with the material straining, and showing their belly-buttons in bas-relief. The leather belt, worn at an imaginary and long-departed waistline, somewhere under the gut, emphasises the story of too much lager and curry and too little exercise and the whole effect shouts 'Slob, wear it under a shirt, or not at all!'

The guffaw. Well, you really need to be in the Far East, where street markets sell T-shirts which have been manufactured and printed by people for whom English is not simply a foreign language, but more like an alien concept. I used to make a mental collection of the howlers that could be seen on the chests of young men and women: 'Enjoy Myself', 'Love and Only is the Important', 'Think Always When Raining', 'Not Be Brind. Look About'. The idea that they sell better if they have something written on them may well have originated in the Orient but it is manifested everywhere in the West so that it is difficult, in England, to find a T-shirt that does not have something fatuous written on it. That is where the irritation comes in: why does it have to have the name of the company you work for, or your local pub, or the college you attended, or the rock group you went to see a couple of years ago, or your bowling/diving/archery/club, or the stag party you went to in Dublin a year or so before, when, in your cups, you all thought that it was hilarious to have 'World Tour' printed on them? Why can't they come, just plain or patterned, without some sort of announcement on them?

And the contempt? Well, what other word better describes the rightful sensation when confronted by a T-shirt which would be quite passable if it were plain and were priced accordingly but which you know has cost very, very much more because it is printed with the name of an exclusive designer and, therefore, the wearer is sending the message that she (yes, probably she) has bought it not because it is comfortable or goes well with the jeans she is wearing or the colour suits her, but because she is proud to be able to afford it. Many Mainland Chinese wear suits with designer labels sewn on the outside of the sleeve and are mocked for their ostentatiousness by Hong Kong and Singaporean Chinese. I see no difference between that and the splattering of the name of a French or Italian fashion house across the chest of Kensington Woman.

There is another form of showing off with the wording on a

T-shirt which, whilst not quite registering so highly on the vulgarity scale, is definitely pitched somewhere between irritation and contempt, and that is the T-shirt with the name of a holiday destination, being worn somewhere else. It is, just, possible to see an excuse for buying an item of clothing which bears the name of your holiday resort. Perhaps the weather was hotter than you had thought it would be, or perhaps, because of the heat, you find that you need to change your shirt more frequently than you had allowed for when you packed. Or, conceivably, the atmosphere of your resort is so captivating that, like a holiday romance, you temporarily ignore the promptings of good judgment and splash out on purchasing something that, at the time, you think you will want to keep forever, to remind you of your passing pleasure. Presumably, though, anyone with any sensibility, when he gets home and unpacks, looks at the object with regret or, at most, as a reminder of a good time, and puts it at the back of a drawer only to be brought out again when the dining-room needs redecorating. It is, I suppose, remotely possible that, in the feeling of flatness that often follows a good holiday and precedes the return to work, and when there is comfort in the contemplation of a return to the same place, you might think that it is worth keeping the t-shirt for next year. However, I fear that I am being far too kind in postulating those motives; the truth is that the purpose of these purchases is not to wear them where they were bought, but to wear them back home or, even worse, on another holiday somewhere else, and that is where you mostly see them.

In the High Street of any Cotswold town in the summer there will be tourists wearing t-shirts emblazoned with the names of resorts in the Caribbean; on the beaches of St Tropez you will see the crimson, peeling faces of Englishmen whose clothing proclaims 'Sydney' or 'Hamilton Island, Queensland'; you come down the steps to the Piazza di Spagna, in Rome and there, sprawled across adjacent seats of a pavement café, is a middle-aged couple from Aberystwyth wearing Australian bush hats and identical T-shirts with something like 'Tropicana Beach Resort, Tenerife' in slightly faded wording. Maybe there was a touch of insecurity in the decision to pack those clothes for a trip to the Eternal City, the feeling that they might make them appear to be the seasoned travellers which their innermost voices told them that they really are not; perhaps they thought that, in this foreign-language land, they might possibly strike up an acquaintance with another couple who were veterans of the Tropicana Beach or that it would be a talking point, rather like those curious metal labels with the names of villages that hikers in pre-war Austria and Germany fixed to their walking sticks, – but, no, I am in danger of unjustified empathy. The reason they do so is to show off, in the belief that the beholder will be impressed. Well, I am not. It is about time that t-shirts were printed with the slogan 'I don't give a fuck where you've been'. I would buy several and pack them for my holidays – except that, in order not to attract smirks, the words would have to be hidden under my shirt.

THE ASPHYXIATION OF ENGLISH

My next attack is on meaningless expressions. Whoever thought of saying "and I quote" before repeating someone else's written or spoken word probably thought that it gave an air of authority, as if vouchsafing for the accuracy of the citation. It is on a par with politicians who introduce a statement with "I am on record as saying", as if that somehow makes their currently expressed opinions true rather than, merely, consistent; and, of course, you can be consistently wrong. The latter hints at his being a personage of such stupendous importance that somewhere, somehow, a record is made of his every utterance. But they are both meaningless (and in the case of 'on the record' often, subsequently, shown to be wrong) and therefore add nothing to what is being said. If something adds nothing, then it conveys nothing and is, therefore, a misuse of the language. One often hears criticism of the way that the ill-educated, whether they be tabloid newspaper readers or writers, speak and write, more often than not directed at lazy pronunciation or the seeming inability of teenagers to speak other than in grunts. But the misuse that I am attacking is perpetrated by people who have, apparently, been well-educated and who, by the use of these phrases, seek to portray themselves as having depth and gravitas.

This is, jarringly, illustrated by an oft-used expression: 'the likes of'. You hear it on the radio and at lectures and see it in newspaper reports. A moment's thought should lead to the conclusion that it really conveys the idea of someone or something like the person or thing who or which is spoken about; what else can it mean? Yet it is employed as if it meant the person or thing itself, as in, 'The charity dance was well-attended with the likes of Pixie Trixie the celebrity, Damien Donut the artist, and the singer-songwriter, Yoric Laser, putting in appearances'. If it was only the likes of them, it ought to mean that the people named were not actually there but, instead, look-alikes went to the ball. I know that some people make a living impersonating the famous so, perhaps, it was they who were there to be seen; but, of course, that is not what is meant at all. It is simply an expression which is the antithesis of what is sought to be conveyed, and it is used for no good reason at all.

Another very good example is rooted on the other side of the Atlantic, but it has begun to make the crossing to these shores. It is almost exclusively used by academics, usually bearded, always wearing glasses and often wearing hairy, tweedy jackets. I have nothing against American academics or beards, spectacles or tweed but my bile begins to effervesce when they use the meaningless term 'if you will', as they do, time and time again as if it adds some sort of learned coda to an assertion which would, otherwise, be indisputable. Perhaps it is also intended to suggest an element of reasonable acceptance of the listener's views by seeking the courtesy of his permission. But it is meaningless and is compounded by pretentiousness; and every time I hear, in a broadcast on a serious subject, something like: "The poet Wordsworth was much influenced by contemporary events in Europe so that he can be described, if you will, as a revolutionary in the context of his time" my foot begins to twitch in the direction of the radio.

A kissing cousin of that conceit is the use of a longer and incorrect version of the word that the speaker or writer means. This, again, is the currency of those who consider themselves well-educated but are not at all sure that others see them in the same light and therefore try to impress with their use of overblown and elongated words. We all have experience of the pompous ass who refers to a pub as a hostelry and a drink as a libation, but this is something different. In the ass's case, he is employing, for effect, a word which, whilst unnecessary, does mean what he intends to say; but, in the instance of which I complain, the word is wrong. Three examples spring to mind: 'methodology', which really means the study or science of method. I once heard a High Court Judge, no less, ask counsel "By what methodology do you intend to establish your case?" Another is 'existential', which means (apart from the philosophical context) 'concerned with human existence', but is used as if it meant 'current' ('an existential threat') or even that difficult word 'is'. The other is 'mechanistic', which means pertaining to mechanism or the study of mechanism, but is often employed to as if it mean mechanical. What is wrong with 'method', or 'existing 'or 'mechanical'? Answer: they don't make the speaker feel impressively erudite.

'Humanitarian', there is another one. It means kindly,

caring, gentle, compassionate, charitable; yet it is constantly and wrongly used as the adjective to qualify the word 'disaster'. How on earth can a bush fire or a famine or severe flooding be compassionate? What the speaker means, of course, is 'human' but it must seem to him that it makes him sound more erudite if he uses a word of six rather than two syllables, even though it is the very antithesis of what he thinks that he is saying.

Examples of the use of overblown language are to be found everywhere. It is now almost inevitable that the description of a job or a trade will hide what it really is and the more humble, the more grandiose the accretion of titles. You might also like to keep a look-out, when you are driving, for a haulage contractor's lorry; it is rare to see one since the business has mostly been transmogrified into 'logistics solutions'.

Back to television and radio journalists for a moment. Why do they persist in saying 'meanwhile' when they don't mean it? That word conveys a period of time between two events, or whilst something is happening. A good if, in my case, unlikely example would be: 'Tomorrow, I shall start digging over the vegetable patch and I hope to finish by the end of the week. Meanwhile would you, please, arrange for me to see an orthopaedic specialist.' Almost as a matter of course, however, they use it as if it means some consecutive or separate event as, for instance, 'Slovakia beat England 12-0 last night. *Meanwhile* Roger Federer won his game against...'. They don't mean meanwhile, they mean nothing; it is just a verbal crutch of the same quality of 'er' and 'umm' – no, it is worse, because it is debasing a real word.

In addition to the meaningless phrase there is the meaningless bolt-on. I can't recall when this started, but I think that it was some time during the last ten years that the habit grew of regularly adding a noun to another noun when the first should apply only in special circumstances. Let me give some examples. There seems to be no such thing as a test any more: it is always a 'litmus test' or an 'acid test'. No-one has a record of doing anything now: he has a 'track record'. And there are so many of them: bench mark, sea change, shell shock, feeding frenzy, food chain (I recently heard a government official talking of 'the educational food chain' when he meant, I think, the different levels of teaching establishments – he certainly was not referring to school dinners). Schools' academic results are so routinely described as 'league tables' that no-one seems to have noticed that, unlike football teams, there is no league to which schools belong. These hackneyed bolt-ons are not limited to nouns. For an example of a bolt-on adjective there is, of course, the depiction of trouble waiting round the corner as a 'ticking time-bomb'. This is particularly juicy because it is also an anachronism. When was a delayed-action bomb last attached to a wind-up alarm clock? Whenever it was, it is probable that the bomb was round and black and the size of a grapefruit and was planted by a man with a wide-brimmed trilby, a cape and a central-European accent. And then there is 'critical mass': when did you last here the word mass being used on its own, other than by a Catholic or a mathematician (or a Catholic mathematician)? Certainly not by a journalist or a politician. It also has the fault of being constantly used erroneously. It is a term from nuclear physics and means the minimum amount of material needed for a chain reaction. It, most decidedly, does not mean a lot of people at a football match, as I have heard it employed by a sports commentator.

Not quite in that category, but worth mentioning here, is the use of the term 'killing spree'. A spree is a lively frolic. Murder should never be equated with boisterous fun. The term is repellent in its inappropriateness, but no more so than that employed by the medical profession for the solemn and sombre process of removing suitable organs from cadavers to be used for transplants. They call it 'harvesting'. Is there anything difficult about the words 'removing' or 'taking'? Another hackneyed expression comes from the word which means something intended to be a pleasurable combination of drinks (actually, it also means a racehorse and a type of beetle, but I do not want to be more than usually pedantic, at least not for the moment). That word, of course, is 'cocktail' and has been used in that sense in America for about two hundred years and in Britain since, at least, the 1920s. If you were to go into the cocktail bar of any smart hotel and ask for a drink you would expect that it might be a mixture of ingredients, but you would not anticipate it harming you or killing you unless, of course, you took it in such quantities that you deserve what is coming to you, in which case you have no sympathy from me whatsoever, and I probably won't even come to your funeral. For some reason, however, the word has come to be used as if it means a mixture and an unpleasant one at that. Actors and singers are routinely described as being found with a cocktail of drugs in them after they have been rescued from some hotel bathroom; and explosive devices are said to be made from a cocktail of ingredients. Actually, it has got worse than that because, the same worn-out adjective is normally attached, so that it is described as 'a *lethal* cocktail'. So, I suppose it means that we will soon have to exercise some caution when we go for a drink and make sure that, when we ask the barman for a cocktail, we specify that it is to be benign. After all, you can't expect the hard-pressed staff behind the bar to remember every time to ask "Will that be lethal or not, sir?"

But a touch of democracy is called for here. Meaningless expressions are not the preserve of the supposedly well-educated. Everyone knows of the insertion of 'like' and 'kind of' and has heard a young and usually female celebrity (of which more, much more, later) relate a moment of surprise, happiness or some other sensation with "I was, kinda, like, wow!", but what I have in mind is the currency of cheap-flight cabin crew and supermarket staff. Bar staff and shops assistants no longer ask what you want or whether they can help; they say "Are you all right, *there?*" Flight attendants lug big plastic bags along the aisle, chanting, "Any rubbish, *at all?*" and I resist the temptation to reply, "No, not even slightly." On flights and in supermarkets and department stores we hear announcements in which every active verb is preceded with the emphasised 'do'; as in: "We DO have a wide range of duty-free items" and "We DO invite you to take advantage of our three-for-the-price of two event which we DO offer on a variety of purchases". It was in a supermarket that the idea of this book came to me.

GASTRO-BOLLOCKS

'Celebrity' chefs irritate many people. Some are fine, and likeable and seemingly modest; but others are over-paid, foul-mouthed, bullying braggarts or irritating know-alls with a faked common touch as they demonstrate their near-impossible creations on television with an unseen team of assistants. They are such an easy target that I think that I will leave them alone. However, it is about time someone had a go at two other culinary species, and I take up the challenge here.

Who are the people who compile recipes for the broadsheet newspapers? Under a heading such as 'A Simple Romantic Supper for Two' they list the ingredients. Some are simple enough: breadcrumbs, butter, self-raising flour, curry powder. But then we get to something like 'two centilitres of fermented yak's milk – I prefer the evening lactation – six grams of Hawaiian candlenut, a pinch each of galangal, ajawan and cubeb (if you can't get cubeb you can use a similar quantity of nigella instead) and ten grams of Ethiopian fenugreek'. There is usually some recognisable meat in the list, but you have to start by frying it until golden brown in safflower oil. Where did they get the idea from that these ingredients were essential or even desirable for the dish? And more importantly, where are you supposed to get them if you don't live near Paddington?

Then there are restaurant critics. There was a time when a

reviewer went, incognito, to have a meal and then wrote an article about it, saying what he had ordered, how well it was prepared and served, whether the wine list was sufficient, what the ambience was like and whether or not he thought the experience to have been good value. He would also give the reader an idea of what he might expect to have to pay; and that was it. It was information of just the kind that you wanted if you were thinking of trying a new restaurant. Such reviews still exist, but normally only in local newspapers and magazines. Critics writing for the national papers have long since abandoned such a useful and modest approach.

Now, if you read a restaurant review it will start with a mini biopic of the reviewer. He will be anxious for you to know how witty and generally superior he is. Almost all the places will be in London (or, quite ostentatiously, in some obscure region of France or Italy which the majority of the readers are unlikely to consider visiting and it is, therefore, merely a dissertation on the gastronomic erudition of the writer) but there will be an occasional foray into some other part of the United Kingdom, in which case there will usually be a sneering reference to some horror, such as that there is cow dung in the countryside or that a skinny mocha-latte seems to be unobtainable in the 'Pig's Head' in Snoring-in-the Wold. After telling you, in wholly unnecessary detail, something of his domestic arrangements and slipping into a personal anecdote which is intended to remind you that he is terribly clever and rather roguish, he will, several paragraphs in, start to tell you about the meal that he has had.

To be fair (as, from time to time, I must) it is here that he starts to say something useful. The description of the interior of the restaurant can be informative, even though you could probably have judged for yourself from the accompanying photograph, and you do read about what was on offer, what he and his guest ate, what the service was like and what he (or rather, his employers) paid. Sometimes the prices seem eye-watering and you are so put off that you would not consider spending such a huge sum on what is, after all, a meal but, by and large, it is at that point that the critic is doing what you want him to do and letting you form your own opinion about whether or not you would like to try the place yourself. There is nothing wrong in doing so in an amusing way, so that the article makes entertaining reading in its own right but, like music and drama criticism, the principal purpose should be to let you know what to expect; if he stopped there, he would have fulfilled that purpose. Unfortunately, he rarely does, and the temptation to show off and, what is worse, to affect knowledge that he does not really possess, is too difficult to resist. He becomes the soul-mate of the recipe writers to whom I have just referred.

Just consider this: a new restaurant opens and it calls itself something like 'Kalipur Spice'. It claims to be the only place in the country specialising in North Andaman Islands cuisine and is soon visited by our food writer. He is in his mid-thirties and has been brought up in, say, Swindon (a fact that he would prefer to keep concealed, now that he has moved to Islington) and has had plenty of experience, in his younger days, of eating in the local curry house. He has been to India twice, the first time as a stopover on a flight to Thailand and the second, quite recently, when he spent a week touring the palaces of Rajasthan. His review of the 'Kalipur Spice' is ecstatic, – he overlooks the uncomfortable seating and the fact that his back has been constantly jostled by the stream of customers collecting their takeaways because, as he puts it, "The cooking is absolutely authentic. The coconut croquettes and the fish *balachao* were cooked exactly correctly although the *bebinca* with which we ended the meal was perhaps slightly sweeter than is normal." Well, I ask, how the hell does he know? The answer is that he doesn't and that he is just assuming that none of his readers will know, either. There is, of course, nothing wrong with saying that he had a very good meal which he thoroughly enjoyed, nor with trying to describe it in terms that his readers might follow; but that is not what he is doing. Instead, he is trying to demonstrate how clever and well-travelled he is. The same applies to reviews of dishes from obscure Chinese regions, central Asian republics, South American tribal areas and, indeed, anywhere. Every time I read the word 'authentic' in a restaurant review, although I am supposed to infer and admire the breadth of knowledge of the writer, my response is 'How do you know, you toss-pot?' or thoughts to that effect.

A particular target of this posturing is Cantonese cooking; the food writer always claims to know the whole range of *dim sum*, say, and precisely what should be in it and how it should be prepared and served and he always knows what current fashion decrees to be the Chinese vegetable *de rigeur*, this week *pak choy*, next week *tung choy* (because that is what happens to be available on the menu) and whether it has been prepared properly. In truth, his knowledge is usually miniscule; unless you have had soya chicken in *Fook Lam Moon* in Wanchai or eaten beancurd from plastic bowls on Lamma Island, how can you gain such omniscience? The answer is: from a couple of meals in a smart Chinese restaurant in Bayswater.

I have spared restaurants themselves from this diatribe. By and large they have cured themselves of clunkingly-awful rubrics, such as 'From the Deep Blue Sea' and 'Baker's Selection', although one does still, occasionally, see 'Chef's Salads' for which explanation we should all be grateful, assuring us, as it does, that the dish has not been prepared by the cleaning staff or the firm's accountant. The irritating words 'drizzled' and 'jus' still make an appearance but subject, of course, to their variable standards, there is not too much to complain of. Except for this; they almost all do it, and I hate them for it: you go into a restaurant without having booked, and ask if they have available a table for two. The response: "Have you a reservation?" Why do they always ask that stupid question? If I had previously telephoned and made a reservation, I would not be walking in and asking if they had a table; I would say something like "Good evening, my name is Wilson, and I have booked a table for two." Why on earth *would* I ask them if they have a table? Perhaps they suspect that people who have booked might keep it secret until, say, the end of the meal, when they compliment the waiter and then let slip that they had made a reservation. No, that cannot ever have happened in the whole history of the restaurant trade. It is a wholly meaningless question. Stop it, now!

Whilst on the subject of eating there is one other piece of idiocy that deserves having a knife stuck into it. This time, it has nothing to do with restaurants, but with the packaging on prepared food that you buy in shops. It might, for instance, be a portion of roast duck with an orange sauce. There is an attractive picture, on the packet, of the duck, in its sauce, on a mound of fluffy mashed potatoes, with some rather nice-looking broccoli on the plate and a glass of red wine beside it. In small wording at the bottom of the picture is the witless message 'Serving Suggestion'. Is it there because, in an age when so much of human activity is informed by defence against possible litigation, someone thinks that the customer might sue if he opens the packaging and finds that it contains no more than what it says on the outside? Do the manufacturers fear letters of complaint: "Dear Sir, I recently purchased your Canard à l'Orange and was appalled, disappointed and shocked to find that it contained no mashed potatoes or glass of claret as illustrated on the package?" Recently, for my lunch, I had some Marks & Spencer chopped herring. I really did not expect the pot to contain the two pieces of brown bread and the sliced-up gherkin which appeared, with the herring, in the picture. So please, Mr M and Mr S, don't lie awake at night worrying that, if you had not printed 'Serving suggestion' I would now be off to the local High Court Registry to issue my writ.

COD SCIENCE

I do not here propose to discourse on ichthyology but the pseudo-scientific words which appear in advertisements, largely but not exclusively, for cosmetics and for yoghurt. The prefixes 'pro' and 're' and the suffixes 'ol' and 'ium' are sprinkled meaninglessly to give a wholly fake aura of scientific-sounding names, in order to suggest that there has been a been a considerable degree of research before the product appeared for sale. The irony is that there almost certainly has been painstaking study, for these days it is practically inconceivable that a reputable manufacturer of anything designed to be put in or on the human body will not have ensured that it is safe to consume or to apply; but by calling a face cream 'pro-rejunvenol' or claiming that it contains 'B-beautifillium' or adding 'ius' to the name of the yoghurt to make the contents of the plastic pot seem to have a special bacterium which is different from, better than, and additional to, that which occurs naturally, simply raises a quizzical eyebrow.

A perfect example is in what has happened to the word 'bifidus'. 'Bifidobacteria' is a real word and connotes a form of beneficial bacterium which exists naturally in the human intestine. Bifidus is said to be a product which promotes the creation of such bacteria and no exception can be taken to the use of that word on its own. However, one international manufacturer of yoghurt has started to tack on the word 'ActiRegularis'; it is wholly made up, and is intended to suggest, presumably, regular bowel action. Of course, it is understandable that the makers of the product would demur from selling what is, after all, a healthy and enjoyable food as if it were a laxative, but what they have done is coyly to hint at that property and wrap it up in a quasi-Latin name suggestive of Linnaean taxonomy. It is all supposed to sound very impressive and to suggest to the purchaser that there is some sort of special ingredient lurking in the pot. But, wait, they must know that it is not only meaningless; it is also faintly ridiculous. How do I know that they know? Because 'Bifidus ActiRegularis' has replaced the former cod-Latin 'Bifidus Digestivum', which was so silly that even the post-adolescent denizens of the merchandise promotion industry must eventually have realised that no-one thought that it could be a serious description.

And how does 'pro-calcium' differ from common or garden calcium? Does it, in some special way, help with the pro-relief and pro-strengthening when you take it with pro-vitamins? Pro-bably not. It is on a par with actors in white coats pretending to be doctors or dentists when they appear in advertisements and recommend some sort of healthful product. Nobody is taken in, unless they are terminally gullible or under five years of age.

ENGLISH A VICTIM OF GRIEVOUS BODILY HARM

Two short moans. First, the 'ee' suffix. When someone does something to or for someone else, the noun representing the latter may end with it, hence a person who puts his house up as security for a loan is the mortgagor and the bank is the mortgagee, and an even clearer example is in instruction, where there is a trainer and a trainee. The rot set in shortly before the Second World War when people who were being offered refuge were, correctly, described as 'refugees'. A misunderstanding may have developed from the fact that they had taken active steps to achieve that status; it was not long before prisoners who had climbed over the wall and legged it were referred to as 'escapees' when they were, manifestly, escapers and whilst at large they came to be called 'abscondees'. This misuse has become so commonplace that nobody seems to notice that the list of those present at a meeting refers to them as 'attendees' (well, I notice, and I object to it). I was once on a bus in the Far East which displayed a notice on the inside saying "Room for 18 Standees". That is obviously wrong and attributable to unfamiliarity with correct English, unless the bus company envisaged some giant hand that would pluck its passengers from the queue at the bus stop and place them either in seats ('seatees' does have a nice ring about it) or in the aisle. But if that one is so obviously funny and wrong, it is strange that 'attendees' arouses so little vexation. Enough of that; I no longer wish to be the writee on this topic.

The other concerns the use of the plural form of a verb with a singular noun. One of the earliest rules of grammar that a child learns is the conjugation of verbs. It is absorbed so easily that it is only when he is still a toddler that he can expect indulgent laughter in response to an error, such as "Mummy are a bootiful lady" or some similarly ingratiating comment. The sole exceptions are the depiction of yokels in formulaic bad fiction, where smock-wearing, rosy-cheeked denizens of some imaginary and impossibly rustic county say "'e be" and "Oi are"; and unfunny portrayals of black people in the Southern States of America, mercifully not now common, but just watch 'Gone with the Wind'. It being such an obvious thing that a singular noun or pronoun takes the singular form of a verb, it is astonishing that the reverse has crept into common usage almost without anyone noticing. It started, I am sure, like so many crassitudes, with sports reporters who think it correct to say "England are drawn against Germany" or "Chelsea have reached the finals". The only explanation for this that I can think of is that these numbskulls think that because a football team (singular) comprises a number of players (plural) the team should be called 'they'. But a wasps' nest is home to thousands of wasps and no-one, assuming him not to be feeble-minded, would say 'a wasps' nest are in my attic'. Now this abuse of the basic rule is everywhere. We hear that 'The government are considering a proposal', that 'Pecksniff plc have announced a loss', and that 'The National Trust intend to oppose a planning application', and I find myself shouting at the radio: "IS!", "HAS!" or "INTENDS!". Just because the government has a number of ministers in it or, in the other cases, shareholders and members, a single entity does not turn into a multiple. We don't say 'France are a republic but the United Kingdom are a monarchy', – well, at least, not yet. Please, get a grip and apply a little common sense before it is too late.

For entirely different reasons, the plural pronoun 'they' and 'their' and the possessive pronoun 'theirs' are constantly misused. This is because political correctness, or sheer laziness, has made it unfashionable to say or write 'his', 'hers' or 'his or hers'. So it is now commonplace to see a sentence such as "When your child is about three years old they should be encouraged to..."Although this is jarring, there is a certain logic, as well as history, to the solecism; but there is no logic to 'When your little girl is about three years old they should be...' yet you see and hear that sort of thing very frequently. So, while you are getting a grip, think about that one, too.

DRAMA CLICHÉS

I am willing to bet that no-one, ever, in real life has concluded a telephone conversation by lowering the handset to chest level and staring at the earpiece[2]. Yet it happens all the time at the theatre and on television. The suggestion seems to be that the character whom you see thinks that he or she will glean some information from it after the other caller has rung off; or, perhaps, the subtext is "Oh no, not my 'phone, surely it couldn't have given me such bad/puzzling/unexpected news. Not the 'phone I have in my house. Has someone substituted it for another one which would tell me such things? I am so bewildered. Perhaps, if I stare at it, all will become clear".

Here's another one. It almost always involves a woman, usually quite young. She has just had a visitor and there has been some sort of tension, not necessarily an argument, it could be a declaration of love or even a piece of more than usually hot gossip. As she close the door after the other person has gone, she turns and leans her back against it. Has anyone, other than an actor, ever done that? I don't find either annoying (so I suppose that this section should not be in this book), but they are puzzling.

---

[2] Oh, alright, I suppose a telephone engineer may have done so. You win.

Car remote locking devices. Now, there is something that I have noticed. Every car I have owned over the last ten or more years has had one, but none of them ever bleeped when I operated them; and nor have I ever heard a sound when other people use them. I suppose that there must be some makes that do that as, after all, it is in the nature of modern gadgetry to emit an irritating noise, but most such zappers do not. Except, that is, in films and on television when there is an inexorable double squeak, rather like a budgerigar with hiccups, when anyone locks or unlocks his car.

DRAMA SOLECISMS

This is something which I do find annoying and is, accordingly, properly in this book.

Some time ago, I gave up buying Sunday newspapers. That was not through parsimony and nor was I trying to save the planet; it was because I was concerned by the prospect of being misinformed. Whereas, on weekdays, the broadsheets mostly contain current news with a fairly small proportion of comment, on Sundays the balance is altered and they concentrate on what they, rather pretentiously, refer to as 'reportage' and authoritative-sounding articles by some self-styled investigative journalist. So often, whenever they touched on a subject which I happened to know something about, such as the law or the Far East or 19th Century history, I could see how ill-informed and, frequently, downright wrong the writers were and it made me realise that I had read much on other topics, about which I had known little before, and probably less afterwards. So it troubles me that, all over the country, otherwise intelligent and well-informed people are being fed imbalanced half-truths and, sometimes, utter rubbish, and upon which they come to opinions on matters of importance and gain false impressions of how things are done, which may or may not be intrinsically important, but which will affect their outlook.

These inaccuracies are by no means limited to journalists.

Writers of non-fiction who cannot take the trouble to check their facts (and I appreciate that I may be leading with my chin, here) also convey errors. I have, for instance, recently read in an otherwise extremely reliable book by a much-respected political commentator that "Derry Irvine gave Blair his first job in legal chambers". No he didn't, only the staff is given jobs in barristers' chambers; the barristers themselves are all self-employed. An example like that, I appreciate, hardly matters and may be forgiven in a long and detailed account of modern history. What does matter is the way that plays and films and, in particular, those made for television, so consistently get things wrong when a little research or, even easier than that, a request for information from someone who actually knows the subject, would get it right.

Anyone who plies a trade or profession which is the subject matter of these productions must go through eye-rolling moments and occasionally suffer explosions of anger at the misportrayal of the environment in which he or she works. Surgeons, soldiers, chefs, airline pilots and practitioners in many other fields can, doubtless, only groan as they watch how, for dramatic effect or from simple ignorance, the realities of how they work are mangled and distorted; but it is the law and, in particular, criminal trials which are especially prone to dramatisation (because of the widely-held misconception that they are all dramatic when the truth is that they are made up of some theatre and much boredom) and it is, therefore, on that topic that I offer five instances of crass inaccuracy.

The first and second concern judges. Because of films and plays and television, people believe that British judges in courts in the United Kingdom have gavels which they strike for attention (or for dramatic effect). No they don't – in the jurisdictions of England and Wales, of Scotland and Northern Island, of the Channel Islands and the Isle of Man (I don't think that I have missed any out) they sit there and, generally, maintain order by the force of their personalities and the fear of committal for contempt of court. In the USA they may very well bang a little wooden hammer, like naughty children trying to attract the attention of their minders, but not here. Nor in the jurisdictions which are close to the English Common Law system, like Australia, New Zealand, Hong Kong, Singapore or Malaysia do they do it and yet, routinely, in all these countries the judge is portrayed, sitting there in his full-bottomed wig, pontificating away, or fast asleep, with a gavel beside him. And that is the second error: they do not wear full-bottomed wigs in court. They are for ceremonial purposes only, when processing for the Lord Chancellor's Breakfast at the opening of the legal year, for instance.

The third also touches on the judge's role in a trial and is far more important. I do not know much about how things are done in America, other than from watching trial scenes in films, which may or may not be accurate, but which show a curious procedure when an objection is taken to a part of the evidence or the form of a question. The attorney who is not asking the questions will be shown, often whilst remaining seated, to shout

"Objection!" or "Objection, – irrelevant!", or some such, and the Judge, without a moment's hesitation, replies either "Sustained" or "Overruled" and the trial proceeds as if nothing had happened. Unfortunately, directors on this side of the Atlantic appear to believe (or more likely, choose to ignore what they know to be true) that much the same thing happens here, only with wigs and gowns on. I have seen it so often and it never fails to make me angry, because it is not only a misrepresentation of court procedure here, it belies the basis upon which our trials work. When counsel in England, or the other places I have mentioned, wants to make an objection he, firstly, rises to his feet and says either that the question is improper, for instance, because it is leading or predicated on evidence that has not been given, or that he objects to the admissibility of this part of the witness's testimony, often giving a brief reason for his objection. In the former case, counsel who has been asking the questions may well concede and not go on to ask the question in that way, or he may disagree, in which case the judge will be called upon to rule, which he may be able to do there and then. If the issue is the admissibility of the evidence, or if it will be necessary to review the evidence that has been given so far, the jury will be asked to leave court, and once they have done so, counsel on either side will set out their arguments and, when they have done that, the judge will give a reasoned decision whether or not he will permit the question to be asked or the testimony to be given. It is all part of our concept of open justice which, amongst other benefits, enables the judge's reasoning to be scrutinised by appellate courts, and it is so fundamental to both the accused's and the public's rights that it is a serious travesty to depict trials here being conducted in such a peremptory fashion.

Which leads me to the fourth. Again, based on a diet of American films, which portray this as commonplace, directors and scriptwriters show court scenes in England (yes, yes, and also Scotland...) which habitually include an interruption in the proceedings where the judge calls counsel to "approach the bench" and there ensues a half-muttered discussion between him and them concerning something of major importance to the trial and, particularly, to the defendant. Well, the Americans may well do that, and viewers may well believe that it happens here but, most emphatically, it does not. There are occasions when counsel in England (yes, I know) may request to see the trial judge in his room, but that has to be for a defined and permissible reason (such as, that the accused is unaware that he is suffering from a terminal illness or that he has co-operated with the police in a way that would put him at serious risk if it were made public and that, therefore, his sentence should reflect his position without anything being said about it in open court); but it is rare for this to happen and, when it does the court short-hand writer or operator of the mechanical recorder will be present to document every word of what takes place.

Finally, there is the gross misrepresentation of how the law of evidence works. Anyone who knows, or who bothers to find out (and one would have, not unreasonably, thought that producers of drama would fall into one or other of those categories) will appreciate that one of the fundamental precepts of English law is that witnesses give evidence of what their physical senses have told them and that is all. Usually it was what they have seen or heard, but it could also encompass what they have smelt or felt. That is why it is called 'evidence' – they testify as to the evident. Other than in the special case of expert witnesses, whose qualification in a particular field – psychiatry or orthopaedic surgery or mechanical engineering, for example – has to be demonstrated to the satisfaction of the trial judge, they are not allowed to offer opinions. In other words, they have to say what happened and not what they thought. In spite of that, regularly, witnesses are shown in film and television drama as expressing their views as if they were taking part in a conversation at a bus stop. I cannot, surely, be the only person, having seen a soap opera murder trial in which prosecuting counsel asked the detective constable in the witness box the question: "And why do you think Maureen murdered her husband?", shout at the television screen "It doesn't happen like that!"

And, I know that I said "finally" but what I have just been dealing with often raises its ugly head in soap operas, and television adaptations of detective stories, such as the works of Agatha Christie and that has reminded me of something else: the reading of the will. Whenever anyone dies in, say, *Eastenders*, the family and various other characters assemble in suitably funereal clothing and big hats in the offices of a solicitor (when he isn't meeting clients in a café or in their kitchens) and they go through the ceremony of The Reading of the Will, which ends with a shouting match (*Eastenders*) or restrained but vitriolic stares at the comely housekeeper who has inherited the bulk of the estate (*Miss Marple*). Except, of course, that nothing like that ever happens. If the family hasn't already learned the contents of the will long before Great Uncle Horace has shuffled off to be with his ancestors, the beneficiaries learn what they have been left by means of a letter from the solicitor who is acting for the executors – very often, he is one of the executors himself. There is no ceremony which involves some oldish fellow wearing a wing collar and half-moon, gold-framed spectacles sitting at the head of a table and reading the will aloud to the expectant and disappointed; there may once have been, for all I know, but if it ever existed it fell victim to the invention of the penny post. It is certainly not part of modern life.

So, why insert these solecisms? They cannot really make for a greater dramatic effect. It would take very little effort to ask someone who is familiar with court procedure (though, perhaps not the habitual criminal) and it would provide a welcome few pounds for some underemployed young barrister if he were asked to cast his eyes over the script for the purpose of adding some verisimilitude or removing some errors and it certainly would not be at all a bad thing if the television and film-watching public were not to be misled about what goes on. Perhaps there is some perverse sentiment that permeates the atmosphere at plot creation sessions, a feeling that it is better to get the details wrong than right. I am mystified by it all; a film director could not actually have been in a court room in England and seen a judge, sitting there with a full-bottomed wig and gavel and, incidentally, saying "Proceed" to counsel for the prosecution, so where has it all come from?

CHEWING GUM

What is it that makes football managers and players, and a host of others, almost always men, think that they look anything other than moronic when they are seen continuously masticating? One would have thought that Rod Steiger's stupendous performance as Police Chief Gillespie in *'In the Heat of the Night'* would have dealt the practice a death-blow. As for chewing gum on the pavement, the speckled surface of almost every town centre looks awful; it is, presumably, very difficult to clean off and, worst of all, is testimony to the fact that hundreds of mouths have spat on the ground where you walk. It is, marginally, less offensive than dog shit. Otherwise, I am all for it.

ENGLISH – A VICTIM OF FORCED FEEDING

The irritating neologism has a long history. In the 1920s or 1930s, for instance, people of a certain social class started using expressions like 'Pleased to meet you, I'm sure' and 'I shouldn't wonder', fairly meaningless expressions which now are to be heard only in old black and white films. They died a well-deserved death, but at least it can be said in their favour that they appeared in common usage for no particular motive or reason. In modern usage, they were organic and do not seem to have arisen artificially. Not so, more recent new words and terms.

The advertising industry is largely, but not entirely, responsible for foisting words on us. That they are unsuccessful (at least in Britain) does tend to diminish the harm to the language but that does not excuse the fact the attempt has been made. The word that immediately comes to mind is 'fragrance' and its made-up, awful past participle 'fragranced'. In every airport duty-free shop and in every advertisement for perfume, the word is thrust at us because, for some reason, advertising agencies have come to the conclusion that it is a good word, indeed, the only word. But outside their procto-contemplative circle, no-one uses it. Have you ever heard a woman saying "I am just going to buy myself a bottle of fragrance?" Of course not. What used to be called 'scent' (there is a word, wonderfully redolent of elderly aunts) became '(eau de) cologne' and then 'perfume' and there was nothing wrong with that because they evolved fairly naturally and people used them effortlessly in ordinary conversation. Evidently, though, they were not good enough; perhaps you can see why in the case of the bombed-out German city and, possibly, scent conjures up an image of dogs sniffing at unpleasant things, but there was really nothing wrong with 'perfume' and the proof of that particular pudding is that that is the word that everyone who speaks English and who is not involved in marketing uses. 'Fragrance' is now, also, the word of choice for air-fresheners. Actually, they are not that at all because they make nothing new or clean or fresh, they simply disguise unpleasant odours by overpowering them with something which is intended, frequently unsuccessfully, to smell better; and when you have installed something that fills your room with a cloying chemical aroma, the claim is that it has been 'fragranced'. Well, it has not: what has happened is that a clammy neologism has been employed to describe the artificial suppression of a smell.

Similarly, with lavatory paper. I know, I know that those of us who smirk at the coy American euphemism 'bathroom' ("He had such a bad tummy upset that he had to go to the bathroom in the woods") are at risk of ignoring the origins of the words 'lavatory' and 'toilet', but 'lavatory paper' is what people call it, or 'loo roll' if they want to sound a touch trendy. However, if you go into a supermarket you will search in vain for anything called lavatory paper; what you have to look for is 'bathroom tissue'. That is what the manipulators now want us to call it. It is possible that they want to distance themselves from the harsh, skiddy products that used to go under those wonderful names, 'Izal' and 'Bronco' and which conjure up memories of carbolic soap and trips to a chilly outhouse at the bottom of the garden, but the more likely explanation is that their false sense of delicacy recoils from the thought of what customers actually do with their products. Fortunately, so far, the linguistic *maquis* has mounted an effective resistance and no shopper yet asks the staff for directions to the bathroom tissue aisle.

AMERICAN PRONUNCIATION OF FRENCH

Here is another puzzle. The United States is a nation built on immigration and it probably has more languages spoken in its homes than any other country on earth. Any urban American is exposed to the sound and sight of foreign languages from childhood – the Hispanic television channels, the Little Italies and Chinatowns, why, New York has a Brazilian quarter – and yet that great nation seems to produce so few people who are capable of even a rudimentary grasp of any language other than English, and, even if they are the first or second generation of immigrants, that of the family's original homeland. If it is due to an innate sense of superiority (much as still lingers on in post-imperial Britain) then it follows that they expect everyone abroad to speak their language, or at least to aspire to doing so. Alistair Cooke, in the 1950s, said that there is a deep-seated belief in the heart of the majority in the United States that everyone else in the world secretly longs to be an American and, if that is still so (and much of the foreign policy of the USA since the end of the Second World War would tend to support that conclusion), then there would not be much incentive to bother to learn anyone else's language. Given that, it is unsurprising that those who do attempt foreign words so often get them wrong or mispronounce them or both, and it is French that seems to be the particular victim. One word encapsulates this and that is '*entrée*' when used in the culinary sense. You would have thought that a pretty good clue to its meaning is given in its proximity to 'entry'. It is the first course of a meal on a French menu. Yet, for some reason that I have never been able to fathom, Americans use it as if it means the main course and that usage has spread so that 'Entrées' appear *after* the starter section on menus all over the English-speaking world. I have seen it in Hong Kong, Singapore, Australia and Britain. What makes it worse is the way they pronounce it. As it happens, the French have the simplest of rules for the stressing of syllables: don't. In any French word all the syllables are given equal stress, except when being spoken by an American who, again, from some inexplicable cause, places a heavy stress on the last syllable. So *entrée* becomes 'onTRAY' and Paris is 'ParEE'. And added to that, is the mangling of pronunciation. Every schoolboy who starts French learns at an early stage that vowels are pronounced consistently, albeit differently, and that 'in' approximates to 'aing'. Americans have decided that it is pronounced 'ong'. So *moulin* becomes 'mooLONG' (as in *rouge*) and *lingerie* becomes not just 'lonjeray' but 'lon-je-RAY', thus creating four errors (think about it) in a word of two syllables.

SAFETY (AND HEALTH)

I do not propose to add my contribution to the argument that society has become too risk-averse for its own good; that case has already been made out, although I do not understand how it is advanced by referring to it as 'Elf 'n' Safety', as the pub wit so often does, unless he thinks that all safety officers are semi-literate Londoners. No, I am going to limit this to one observation and one story, both of which concern hard hats.

The observation is this: almost every outdoor activity, other than sport and sunbathing, is shown on television with someone wearing a hard hat. Of course, it is quite right that, in some situations, as in a quarry where explosions are likely, hard hats should be obligatory. But when the Mayor of Lower Piddlington takes part in a ceremonial planting of a sapling in a local park to commemorate some anniversary or other, he always appears in his suit, with his gold chain of office hanging round his portly shoulders, with a new, gleaming spade in hand, and a hard hat on his head. You see people taking part in an archaeological dig, in some wild and remote open space, squatting in or kneeling by trenches which are only inches deep and they all have on hard hats. One irritating presenter, who runs around between these trenches and breathlessly pretends that there are only three hours left to find what has been buried for centuries, will be seen being driven in a 4x4 to the next location, wearing his hard hat *in the car*. It used to be thought of a sign of *machismo* to have a hard hat on the rear shelf of your vehicle but that, surely, cannot be the reason for the current proliferation of yellow headgear. No, it is a bizarre take on safety gear. Which leads me to the story.

For a period before the change of sovereignty in 1997, I had an apartment in the Admiralty district of Hong Kong. It was in a very tall block and my flat was on one of the upper floors. It overlooked a site where the new British Consulate was being constructed in readiness for the handover. Rapidly, it began to rise from the ground, girt in the bamboo scaffolding and green netting which are still used there even for the erection of skyscrapers. Bare-chested construction workers swarmed over the scaffolding with a sure-footedness and confidence that seemed to owe little to safety equipment and much to an exhilarating enthusiasm to get the job completed. One early summer evening I came back home to find that all the scaffolding had been dismantled and carted away, the tower cranes had gone and, in their place, a building stood across the road; it was just below the level of my lounge windows and I could see that it had even got to the stage of the installation, on the flat roof, of the tracking for the bogey from which the window cleaners' cradle would eventually be suspended. The next evening, and there were signs that the topping-out ceremony was imminent. Chairs were laid out in rows on the roof, and an elevated dais had been erected. I came back, especially early, the next afternoon, to find that the ceremony was underway. A number of dignitaries, local and expatriate, where seated on the chairs, a huge floral display and a glazed, roast pig, bedecked with Chinese good fortune symbols, had been placed on a trestle in front of the dais and, standing on the dais, was the British Foreign Secretary, apparently making a speech. When he finished, he stepped down from the podium and walked past the pig to a doorway, where he cut a wide, red silk ribbon which was stretched across it. I could see, but not hear, clapping. It was a charming scene, both gentle and significant, because it was a harbinger of the end of Britain's status in Hong Kong and of its colonial history and it boded well for the future because, among the applauding dignitaries I could make out the faces of several prominent members of the Administration of the People's Republic of China. It was a touching moment, spoiled, almost utterly, by the ludicrous fact that the Foreign Secretary, the Chinese officials and all the others (except for the pig) were wearing hard hats. They were at least forty floors up and there was nothing above them. The only thing that might have possibly passed overhead would have been a Boeing 747 and, had it fallen on them, well, I don't suppose that a helmet would have provide much protection.

THE INFECTION OF ENGLISH

This is not so much a complaint about bad English as a protest against the adoption of some Americanisms which contribute nothing. There are so many instances of imports from other languages that have enriched ours, that it would be worse than ungenerous not to acknowledge them and worse still to object to them on the sole ground that they are not originally part of a language whose very splendour comes from its gathering so much from elsewhere. Indeed, there are many examples of pithy, catchy, cogent expressions that have come from across the Atlantic and have established themselves, comfortably and usefully, in British usage. Moreover, as far as I am concerned, the inhabitants of the USA can, mostly, do what they like with their version of English; but if they come up with some trite or meaningless expression, those of us who care about the way the language is used here have, I believe, a justified grievance when it slips into ours. There was a time, quite a long time, when English singers of popular songs affected an American accent in the belief that they sounded more modern, trendy and, therefore, attractive. It lasted from the 1940s until the native sound of Liverpool burst onto the scene. Looking back, now, these fake Yank accents seem ludicrous; yet much the same thing is current with the written and spoken word as expounded by the press and broadcasters. An example is 'Go Figure!' It is an ungrammatical and unattractive expression of bemusement and it does not fill any void, because there are so many useful, common expressions that mean the same thing, such as, 'Work that one out'. Yet it is being thrust at us with increasing frequency and for no obvious reason other, perhaps, than that the speaker thinks that by using it he will sound urbane, perhaps that it will give the impression that he has actually (and, here, I'm kinda like, wow!) been to the USA! The real effect is the opposite from that intended: he just sounds like an arsehole. Another is 'cheated on'. This may have its origin in the American tendency to euphemism, in order to give a certain distance, when it is used, from the physical details of an unfaithful sexual relationship but, if a discreet term is needed, there are plenty of them in current English. We are all used to the term 'had an affair with' and we all know what it means. So, why use a verb that connotes fraud, or swindling at games? If Americans want to adopt that expression for adultery, let them. It is their business. When a broadsheet newspaper such as 'The Times' has started using it, as it has, then we should object.

I referred earlier to college campuses in the United States from where the rules of what is and what is not acceptable appear to emanate. Some of it strikes most of us as sheer nonsense, but it is their nonsense, and it is the responsibility of discerning Americans to deal with it there. It is when an attempt is made to impose them on us that it becomes offensive and we have the right and, I think, duty to object. There are so many examples, but let me start with one which, undeniably, come from the USA, and that is the term 'African-American'. I know that this is a sensitive subject, but there is no reason why it cannot be dealt with considerately. The problem, of course, is that these politically-correct expressions are always coined in a display of concern for those deserving of compassion, or who are perceived to be at a disadvantage, and these arrogant dictators of language bank on the reluctance of decent people to give offence to such groups by challenging their neologisms. There has always been a dispute about what to call people who are descended from the victims of slavery. The term 'negro' was once used as a perfectly inoffensive classifier, but it has fallen out of use, probably because it was the source of a deeply unpleasant term of abuse. 'Coloured' was originally a description adopted by people whose motives were impeccable: hence 'The National Association for the Advancement of Colored People' but that, too, came to be regarded as, if not insulting, at least condescending. Then there was 'Black', a word which was so acceptable that even those who descended from different ethnic groups were happy to use it, as, for instance, in Britain, the National Black Police Officers Association. That, though, was not good enough for some campus tyrant who decided that the term to be used was now 'African-American', little knowing that more than eighty years earlier, H.L.Mencken had coined the sardonic word 'Aframerican'. It is a meaningless adjective, because most black Americans have never been to Africa. I know it causes resentment in those it purports to protect because, when I was last in New York, I read an article in 'The Herald Tribune' by a journalist who strongly objected to it on the grounds that she and her parents and her grandparents were born and bred in the USA and who wanted to be described, simply, as an American. She was quite right; these hyphenated descriptions do nothing for social cohesion. Why not say, for instance, 'American Jews'? Jewish-American, does nothing except to suggest a qualification of the status, as if they are not, ('well, you know… not in the sense of our Country Club membership, if you will') quite like us.

On the subject of ethnicity, how could they have got the word 'native' so wrong? Anyone with a modicum of education knows that it does not mean aboriginal or indigenous, but having been born in a certain place. Don't they see where the word 'nativity' comes from? When I was young, the word was used by a certain type of Englishman to describe anyone with a skin colour different from his own, in other words, non-white, but now most sensible people use the word in its proper sense so that anyone, of any racial background, can properly be called a native Londoner or a native Frenchman (well, of course, not anyone, he or she has to be born there, but you knew perfectly well what I mean). You can understand why the term 'Red Indian' might be considered objectionable – they are, after all, no more red than the Chinese are yellow, but to substitute for it the term 'Native American' is to bring together both a linguistic solecism and an echo of the colonialist era. What would happen if a Cherokee couple, no longer able to tolerate living with the politically-correct destruction of the language, emigrated to, say, Luxembourg and had a family there? Would the self-appointed arbiters still insist on referring to their children as Native Americans, even though they were native Luxembourgers? I am not sure that I can suggest a decent alternative to Red Indian, although, if you have to classify people, 'American Indian' seemed quite a good way of doing it; not though, good enough for the despots of pseudo-empathy.

It must have been from America that the expression 'learning difficulties' came. What an odd way of describing a disability. We don't talk about the limbless as having walking difficulties or the blind as having seeing difficulties. It is not just that it is a clunky expression for cognitive or mental problems; it is a serious misdirection of meaning, for whilst those to whom the expression is attached may well (although *not* necessarily) have problems with acquiring knowledge and skills, so do many people within the normal range of intelligence, in respect of particular areas. Many people have no aptitude for mathematics or foreign languages, for example, and can properly be described as having difficulties in learning them. I know that it sounds very unsympathetic even to set foot in this territory, but that cannot be helped if we are to stand up to the language bullies. Some of the old terms were, at best, insensitive and it is good that they have gone; but to impose 'learning difficulties' in substitution for, say, 'mental disability' is to do nothing for those whose deserve our understanding and sympathy.

The ludicrousness of this trend was recently demonstrated by guidance (and whilst on the subject of such guidance, why has the noun 'advice' been replaced with adjective 'advisory'? – "The Department of Transport *have* issued an *advisory* on the adverse driving conditions") from a government department to its employees that the term 'disabled' was no longer to be used and that, instead, 'persons with a disability' must be used. What on earth do they think the difference is – other than that it takes slightly longer to say?

FIRST NAMES

You note, I do not say 'Christian names', not for reasons of political correctness but because we live in a multi-cultural, multi-creed society and many people do not have baptismal names. I suppose that I am in error even to use the term 'first name' because in many countries of the Far East, it correct to use the family name first and even as close to home as France, it is conventional in formal correspondence to address someone in the reverse order to that to which we Anglophones are accustomed; but you know what I mean – personal names.

Obviously there is nothing wrong with personal names. Everyone (except Inspector Morse) needs one and, just as life in a society without surnames, such as Iceland, would be full of particular difficulties (and, yes, I have looked at the telephone directory in Reykjavik), so would life without first names. However, like most people of my generation, I was brought up to use them only for friends, acquaintances, family, children, animals and, I suppose, monarchs and saints. Seemingly, almost overnight, surnames took a back seat, and now you are addressed by people whom you have never previously met, or heard of, by your first name. You are telephoned out of the blue by your bank or your insurance company or by someone trying to sell you double-glazing, or you receive a letter from the dealer who sold you a car three years ago, and it never seems to occur to them that you should be called 'Mr or 'Mrs' or whatever title or honorific you might normally use. It is, I suppose, now a lost battle; to say "I beg your pardon, I don't believe we have actually met" labels you as a pompous ass in the eyes of the other person and so, rather than run that risk, you grit your teeth and quietly resolve to resist whatever it is that he or she may be offering.

It all came about because there was an understandable desire to abandon unnecessary formality. Nobody, except the terminally fusty, concludes a letter these days with "I beg to remain your most obedient servant"; and referring to the last, the current and the next months as 'ult', 'inst' and 'prox' has been abandoned with little lamentation. But like so many commendable concepts, informality has gone too far in the direction of mateyness in inappropriate circumstances, so that we have had a Prime Minister who referred to himself as 'Tony', a Leader of the Opposition called 'Ed', prominent politicians who are always 'Nick' and 'Vince', a Director of Public Prosecutions who was known, officially, as 'Ken' and a Lord Chancellor who signed letters from his office 'Charlie'. For Heaven's sake, we are not, all of us, their friends. The result is that, far from feeling a glow of affection for the warmth of their personae, you have something more than a suspicion that they are fakes. I suppose that the one thing that can be said is that it has ironed out an unjustifiable gender inequality; in offices, for instance, women were much more likely to be addressed by their first name than men, in a remnant of that pre-enfranchisement epoch when they were treated rather as children were, but I cannot think of much else in favour of this over familiarity.

Curiously enough, it also seems to be believed that everyone should know everyone else's first names, as though they could not, otherwise, function. Take this as an example: you board a plane and settle down for your ninety minute flight; you expect some sort of welcome over the loudspeaker system and the odd announcement and a run through of the safety drill; but none of this can start until you are given the names of the pilot and the first officer (which may be intended to reassure you that there are, at least, two competent drivers in the cockpit and, therefore, I don't complain about that) and the first names of all the cabin staff. Why? What conceivable reason is there for the passengers to know that 'the cabin service director' is called 'Tracy' and that she is assisted by 'Stacey' and 'Lacey' and by 'Armando', the tinted-haired hermaphrodite (well, she doesn't announce that description, but you soon work out who Armando is)? Am I the only passenger who says to himself "I don't need, or even remotely want, to know your names. Just get on and serve the drinks"? Probably, I am.

It has spread to television announcements. Latterly, the main channels have taken to airing very short news bulletins, under some such rubric as '60 Second Update', the first few moments of which are taken by the, invariably, very young woman newsreader saying "Hi, I'm Samantha Wotsit". Similarly, with weather forecasts. Even television advertisements are now often introduced by someone giving his or her name, for no evident reason other than, perhaps, to add a degree of veracity to the spiel. If that is the case, it does not work. You are not endorsing a product because you perceive yourself to be famous and would like us to buy it because you seem to approve of it; you are doing it because you're being paid, just like the genuinely famous actor whose voice-over is meant to be recognised; but you're not famous, you are a nonentity and both you and the ad makers have convinced yourselves that it will sell better if you tell us your name. You are all fooling yourselves.

NODDING POLITICIANS

We have all seen them, on the front benches of the House of Commons (but, curiously, not in the House of Lords) or during the party conference season. A minister is making an important speech or answering a question from an opponent and, on either side of him or her, like those toy dogs that you used to see just inside the rear windscreen of the car in front of you, his colleagues sit there vigorously wagging their heads up and down. It is not a natural reaction; it is a piece of artifice, intended to demonstrate support, and looking about as genuine as the spontaneous eruptions of joy from the crowds attending the speech of a North Korean Leader. The test is this: would they do it if they didn't think anyone was watching them? Of course not. So, please, stop it. None of us are taken in by it, not your political opponents nor your supporters nor those of us watching you in the audience or on camera.

THE CULTURE OF CELEBRITY

I am not certain why this is commonly referred to as 'The Cult of Celebrity' as 'cult' means a branch or form of religious worship, often with a particular person as the current leader or as the object of devotion. Perhaps it is, mistakenly, taken as an abbreviation of the word 'culture', which seems to be more apposite. However, that is by the by.

I have touched on so-called celebrities before. Of course, there are sportsmen, actors, chefs and artists who are very famous and who appear at glittering gatherings of the rich and renowned and there are some, a few, who shun the limelight but who, nevertheless, are known to millions, but there are others who are described as celebrities because there is no other label to put on them, lacking, as they do, any discernible talent. Some of these are best known for pouting and posing and getting arrested, or for having inherited huge wealth; others are known because they had a brief relationship with a footballer or football manager, or because, after unsuccessful careers as models, they have courted as much publicity as they can for the sort of details of their private lives which most sane people would be embarrassed to disclose to their closest friends. These people thrive on, and perpetuate, the concept of 'celebrity' as an end in itself; they employ publicists to ensure that their shallow, sequined lives are as constantly exposed to public view as is possible and the result is that the front pages of several tabloid newspapers are more often filled with stories of the trivia of their activities than with news of genuine importance and public concern.

The usual and facile answer to this is: "Well, it's all harmless and they wouldn't be able to sell these stories if no-one bought the papers that published them." But that is not true: it is not harmless, because youngsters are being led to believe that being a 'celebrity' is a desirable end in itself, considerably more praiseworthy than being a carpenter or a doctor or a shopkeeper or a proper actor or a musician. It is not now uncommon, when asking young teenagers what they want to become when they leave school, to hear that all they want is to be famous. Moreover, because these celebrities are treated as objects to be admired and envied, their infidelity and immorality, their drug-taking and dishonesty are regarded as normal or, at least, acceptable. So, television programmes proliferate with titles including the word 'celebrity' or, more usually, 'Celebrity' and, in the case of one of them, the only claim that a participant could make to any form of prominence was that he had served a sentence of imprisonment for fraud. It is absurd to claim that there is no harm in it when the young are encouraged to admire the very qualities that damage society. As for the assertion that no-one would buy newspapers if they were not interested in the contents, that wholly ignores the fact that newspapers try to lead and to influence opinion rather than merely reporting the news; why else, before every general election, do they pronounce their verdicts on who their readers should vote for?

Finally, there is this: one often hears complaints of a dumbing down of society. This trend started unquestionably in America but it has rapidly spread to Britain, Australia and elsewhere; so that we are alerted to the fact that a packet of nuts may contain nuts, and are warned, after watching a tight-rope walker, or a demonstration of fire-fighting equipment, not to 'try this at home' or, at the end of an episode of a soap opera, when a deranged, alcoholic Neanderthal has been banned from the local pub after threatening a couple of gay men with a sub-machine gun, we are informed that "if you have been affected by any of the *issues* in tonight's programme" there is a helpline to call. But that is all, at most, irritating. The really insidious and damaging form of dumbing down is the lionisation of seedy nonentities, because it lowers standards for aspiration to the level of the meagre abilities of these 'celebrities' and because, as a consequence, it treats true achievements as if they were not worth the effort.

UNCONTROLLED CHILDREN

It does not seem so long ago that pubs in Britain were where you went to meet adult friends and have a drink and a talk, and departure lounges at airports all over the world were where you waited, in varying degrees of discomfort, before you boarded your plane. Now the principal function of both appears to be as crèches for rampaging children whose parents seem to have forgotten their existence. Even the children who are young enough still to be in pushchairs within reach of their minders yell for attention, as if they could possibly have gone unnoticed in their enormous conveyances, which seem to have been produced by an armaments factory which, having completed an order for Centurion tanks, has diversified into child carriages in order to make use of the left-over components.

CHARITIES

Many of us have come across fake 'hard luck' stories: the man who approaches your car at a service station and says that he has discovered that he has left his wallet at home, or the well-dressed 'student' who has had his pocket picked and who needs to borrow the train fare home and, if only you would be kind enough to give him your name and address, he will be sure to send you the money you have lent him. It is, also, not unknown to receive in your mail a request for a donation from some wholly bogus organisation which, usually in the name of the Lord, entreats you to send an offering to ease the suffering of non-existent victims of hardship somewhere in Africa. I have had all of that and I have also had my way blocked, in a London street, by a thuggish-looking man rattling an indecipherable tin who sought my contribution for 'the homeless'. These are, of course, all crimes of one kind or another because they are attempts to get money by deception and they are dishonest. No-one would suggest that real charities would be guilty of dishonest behaviour, would they?

Well, how about this? As Christmas approaches there is a marked increase in mailings from respectable charitable organisations. No doubt, they think that, as it is the season of goodwill, and that, as those fortunate enough to be able to afford to contemplate the annual round of expenditure on gifts and gluttony might be more than usually liable to be troubled by their consciences when reminded of those who are not as well-blessed by providence, there is more likely to be a positive response to a request for a donation than at other times of the year. There is not much wrong with that; they are legitimately taking advantage of an opportunity that presents itself, and it is so well-established as to be part of the seasonal tradition. However, it goes further. Most big charities now run themselves like commercial operations and they spend a sizeable chunk of the donations they receive – money sent with the intention of alleviating suffering – on paying for the services of marketing consultants and other forms of 'communicators' and, no doubt, it was these professionals who observed that, as well as being the season of munificence, it is also the time when most people are very busy. In almost all jobs, it is a time of stress with the rush to fulfil obligations by Christmas; it is when VAT and income tax returns have to be worked on; it is when the approaching new year means all sort of administrative actions have to be taken; and, above all, when personal time is occupied with trying to decide on, locate and then buy the right presents for members of the family and colleagues, whilst trying not to replicate last year's gifts, as well as with the logistical problem of which in-laws to invite or visit on which day without having a rerun of the internecine conflict that made the break-up of Yugoslavia seem relatively civilised. It is, in short, a time when you are most likely to forget whom you have made contributions to in the past and are least likely to search through cheque stubs and credit card statements.

So what do many of these charities do? They write to you, having obtained your name and address from a list broker, and pretend that you have donated in the past. The letter will, typically, be addressed 'Dear Supporter' and go on to tell you how much your valued contributions over the years have helped in their worthy cause. They are too subtle to make an outright suggestion that if you fail to continue to make a payment you will jeopardise their work, but they bank on the likelihood that the reaction of decent people will be: "Oh well, if I have made donations previously I had better not stop now". The fact that you have never supported them before will, in this time of pressure, escape you. It is only in that comparatively rare circumstance when the charity is one to which you know you have never contributed, because of some religious or political objection or because you have been struck by how much more deserving other fund-raising organisations are, that you realise that this is an insidious attempt to get money from you. It cannot be explained away as some sort of error; large charities these days have computerised records and they know, when sending out their mail shots, who are their past and regular donors, and who are not. It is, quite simply, a deliberate deception.

There is something else that some charities do which, whilst not amounting to dishonesty, has a tinge of blackmail, albeit of the emotional rather than the menacing kind. I am not referring to the display of pitiful and disturbing photographs of people suffering from malnutrition or the depiction of children suffering from cruelty and sexual maltreatment, for there is nothing wrong in forcing people to confront discomforting realities with the intention of alleviating suffering. What I have in mind is something that, at first blush, seems to be so trivial as to be hardly worth mentioning, or worth taking the trouble to do something about but which, because it has become so widespread a practice, really does need stopping. It is the sending of an unsolicited gift to accompany a request for a donation. Homes all over the country have drawers which rattle with cheap ball-point pens that have been sent in the post by some charity or other. You receive small packets of tawdry Christmas cards, or plastic bracelets, or little metal brooches or a trinket supposedly made by African schoolchildren. One very well-established and otherwise praiseworthy institution sends several pages of adhesive labels printed, without your request or permission, with your name and address. Some charities even send a small sum of money, a few copper coins sellotaped to their letters without, seemingly, noticing the irony that the contents of the letter point out how little it costs to provide seed corn, or clean drinking water, or education in the poverty-stricken community for which they are soliciting donations. I do not know if I am unusually hard-hearted in that my reaction to these gifts is reluctance to send any money in response. I do not like the attempt to impose a moral obligation either to send the tat back (which they bank on scarcely anyone doing) or to make some sort of payment and, equally, I do not want the donation which I make for a benevolent purpose to be used for anything other than that purpose and the *necessary* cost of administration. I object to its being spent on offerings to those who are not in need, and I object equally to its being spent on the fees and salaries of the people who come up with these daft, meretricious ideas.

There are many charitable organisations that shrink from such duplicity and, spend their funds wisely; but there is a significant section of the big names which do not. You know who you are.

CUDDLY TOYS

Of course I am not opposed to soft toys *per se*. They are wonderful for small children and it is quite engaging to see how teenage and older girls often continue to treasure the favourite which (one could almost say, who) comforted them from their early years, and still have an honoured place on the bed or dressing table. They are symbolic of contentment and comfort. But it is not comfort that they have come to represent when left at the scene of a fatal road accident or propped against the wall of a house in which someone has died in circumstances which hit the news.

We used to be a nation which tended to minimise outward displays of emotion. Whether that was a good thing or not is arguable, but what has come in its place is distinctly unpleasant. It is sometimes called 'The Princess Diana Effect' but I think that is wrong, because, for an appreciable time before August 1997, it had become acceptable to manifest feelings of joy or sadness as if performing for an audience – her death merely brought that into sharper focus with the thousands, if not millions, of floral tributes from people who had never met her but who, nevertheless, were described as 'mourners'. Amongst the ocean of flowers outside Kensington Palace in that hot summer period there was the puzzling presence of a few teddy bears. Flowers have long been associated in Western society with the ritual of demise, particularly at funerals, and whilst quizzical eyebrows might have been raised at the sight of monuments to the war dead in towns all over the country being piled high with bunches of flowers after the death, in a car crash, of a beautiful, troubled woman, at least the nature of the tribute was understandable. But where did the idea of teddy bears come from? It was not as if this was the death of a small child, when such an offering, even though mawkishly maudlin, would have some sort of connection; this was a woman in her mid-thirties and a mother. I don't know whether her death started the trend or whether it had been happening before, but now it is in full, syrupy flood.

At every crash site, outside every house where there has been a fire, against the railings of every school which the pupil attended, as long as someone has died, there will be bunches of flowers and, ever increasingly, fluffy rabbits, teddy bears and other soft toys, regardless of whether or not a small child was involved. If that were not enough, this gagging over-sentimentality has broadened to include, of all things, brightly coloured metallic balloons, often with a Disney-like animal face with bows and streamers attached, so that the scene of a tragic death is no longer marked by a sombre display of sadness and distress but has been transformed into something like a macabre birthday celebration. It is more than puzzling why this phenomenon should have taken hold and I can venture only a diffident explanation: ever since tragedies like the Penlee lifeboat disaster in 1981, a sense of guilt developed among the overwhelming majority of us who leave it to the minority to put their lives and wellbeing at risk in trying to keep the rest of us safe; that guilt developed both into the belief that we would feel better if we gave money to the dependents of those who died protecting others, and from that developed the idea that we must all be shown to be deeply affected by any death, so long as it occurred in newsworthy circumstances. As a result, if that is right, people are anxious to display a sign of the grief which they believe that they ought to feel (hence the large writing on the labels attached to the flowers and toys to identify whoever placed them); and the more garish, the more conspicuous their offering will be. Like with so many things, there is a sense that you must do what you think others will do; and it has become an ostentation, a sort of competition of emotion.

Whether that hypothesis is right or whether there is another explanation for this phenomenon, the result is the same: what was once the decorous laying of a wreath as an expression of condolence has become a tasteless ritual where dignity is replaced by the tacky, the excessive, and the horribly inappropriate.

SLOGANS AND TAGLINES

I have to admit to a slight, if slightly perplexed, admiration for a group of people who seemed to have thought long and far into the distance and created decent livings for themselves without creating anything or performing any discernibly useful service. When I was growing up and approaching the age when you had to start thinking about work after your education had finished, the choices were, roughly, four-fold. The academically brighter boys considered some sort of profession like law or medicine or accountancy, the artistically-inclined gravitated towards music or the arts or journalism, the technically competent were expected to do something which would require manual dexterity, and others considered following their fathers into, say, insurance or shop keeping. I did not know anybody then who had the vocation to do something totally pointless and earn money from it. I suppose we were all too unimaginative, or were driven by the sense that lingered on for many years after the war, and after National Service had been abolished, that we really had to get on and do something useful, whether it was making furniture or drafting wills or driving buses or treating the sick.

Somewhere along the line, when boys of my generation had long been hard at work, someone must have realised that there was gold to be mined in persuading institutions that they needed a slogan or tagline. The skill which I, slightly, esteem is not manifested in the slogans themselves, for they are universally crass, but in the promotion of the idea that, not only do they have some point but, also, that they are worth paying for. There must be quite a trade, for you see them everywhere, stating the obvious or the incomprehensible. Here are three examples:

The Department of Transport: "Working to deliver a transport system which balances the needs of the country".

The Royal Orthopaedic Hospital, Birmingham: "Delivering same-sex accommodation. Mission accomplished".

The Department of Work and Pensions: "Work, welfare, wellbeing, well delivered".

Three things stand out. The first is the frequent use of the gerund, as in the first two examples, the result being: Creating an ungrammatical sentence. The second is the doing (correct use of the gerund) to death of the verb 'deliver', a word which connotes taking something somewhere, when 'provide', surely would be more apt. The third is the sheer pointlessness of it all; yet stationery and signage and websites abound for public bodies and private businesses which more often have them than not. Somebody must think that it is really a good idea to state the obvious and to pay someone to design it, and someone else to paint it on signboards – and nobody seems to question it: why, for instance, "Spotting speeders in Essex" is part of the local police website, or in what way it aids the enforcement of the law?

Nowhere seems safe from the urge to give off a whiff of insincerity by hanging the identity of your organization on a worthless slogan. Even in the dignified curtilage of one of the Inns of Court, a set of barristers' chambers published a brochure some years ago describing it as "A niche player in a niche market". Even when matters of momentous international importance occur, the image-makers are brought in, so that the invasion of Iraq in 2003 appropriated a term which had been coined a few years earlier and was given the tagline 'Shock and Awe' as if it was some Hollywood Blockbuster. Was a single military decision affected or effected by it? Was a life spared or an enemy made to yield because of it? No; it was all part of the merchandising of every aspect of human activity and was, seamlessly, followed by the 'Pack of Cards' by which the public (that is to say, the American public) was intended to be persuaded that the capture of Iraqi political and military leaders by an invading army was a simple and justifiable affair, as normal as a game of, say, poker, or Happy Families.

When Churchill said "From Stettin in the Baltic to Trieste in the Adriatic an iron curtain has descended across the Continent", he spoke with dramatic imagery. It was a tellingly descriptive term which slipped easily into common usage. When George W Bush repeatedly used the expression 'Axis of Evil' it became a catchphrase and, like an advertising slogan, it was debased and, with repetition, became meaningless. Now that we see slogans and taglines everywhere, painted on the sides of lorries, printed beneath the names of public bodies, even "Fair, Fearless, Effective" on the home page of the Crown Prosecution Service website, the question has to be asked: is that what you are, or just what you aspire to be? The CPS would be wise to think of dropping that slogan or substituting it for something a little more realistic (and it could even use the gerund) like "Trying to achieve just results in difficult financial circumstances and in spite of a shortage of effective in-house lawyers" or even "Doing our inadequate best". Now, there's a tagline that might make people take notice.

HEROES

Apart from the proper names of a mathematician from Alexandria and of the tragic lover of Leander, 'hero' means someone of exceptional courage or, in literature and drama, the main character (so long as he is not also a villain). Acts of great bravery and personal sacrifice are cheapened by the constant use of the word when referring to the exploits of soccer players and rock musicians, as if the valour of R.A.F. pilots during the Second World War was no greater than some grossly overpaid and over-publicised Premier League striker.

I believe that 'hero' also refers to a heavily stuffed, cheesey American sandwich. Perhaps that is what they mean.

SOCIAL NETWORKING

It is very easy for people to bemoan the passing of traditions and social mores and, perhaps, no-one is more prone to do so than someone who has found the time to write a book like this. The developments in technology have been astounding recently and even the newly-retired curmudgeon cannot turn his face from reality and must, if he is honest, acknowledge how wonderful and useful it is to be able to send and receive photographs, to book theatre tickets, to check the long-range weather forecast, to identify the source of a quotation or to settle an argument, by using the internet. And I suppose that there might be something to be said for the facility with which you can instantly share your half-formed, inconsequential thoughts with a wide group of acquaintances – if, that is, you are a thirteen-year old schoolgirl. However, civilisation can hardly be said to have advanced when grown-up people of full mental capacity follow and share with each other the trifling minutiae of their lives. "I'm off to bed now", "I really, really love Yorkshire pudding"; "I've got a headache, but I had too much red wine last night"; "I'm not looking forward to going to work tomorrow"; "I've just got off the 'plane at Heathrow, rotten flight"; "England are never going to win with that line-up", "Why do you say that?", "Cos they're rubbish"; "Hurrah for curry".

It is not that it doesn't matter. It does; all this twittering and twattering has made it not only acceptable, but normal, for inchoate thoughts, which should have been left unexpressed, to be uttered, communicated and stored forever. It is the very antithesis of the reflective process which precedes written communications such as letters and emails, and it encourages an egocentrism in which every pointless idea and every sensation and impression is deemed worth sharing with others.

Where in the social network scheme of things is there room for silent reflection, the pause before deciding to commit what passes through your mind to expressing it? I used to think that it was a peculiarly American trait to utter aloud (very aloud) every trivial thought and observation – "Gee, that's a big cow", "Look, Honey, another McDonalds", – but that is not now correct; it's being done everywhere by social networking. It is common enough to say to people with a seemingly pathetic lifestyle that they should get out more. Well, precisely. That way you might lose some weight, avoid the risk of Vitamin D deficiency, and improve your mind and your social proficiency.

ROAD SIGNS (AND OTHER SIGNS)

I am using this as a lead in to a much more serious gripe. My starting point is that road signs can drive you mad; either because, on a dual carriageway, they are often so placed that, although you know that one is there because you have seen it as a distant shape, as you get close enough to be able to read what it says you cannot actually do so because there is a line of slow-moving lorries between you and it; or because, on country roads, you progress by direction signs for an intermediate town or village, only to find that, when you get to a T-junction, the signs indicate several other places in either direction, but not the one that you have been following.

That, though, is nothing compared with what happens when you are on the M40 or any other major road going westwards and, suddenly, all the signs are in Welsh and English, and given equal space (although, to my untutored eye, Welsh words seem to take up a lot more space than English). If you are not a Welsh-speaker, it comes as a slight shock and, at the least, a distraction to be confronted by wholly unfamiliar words, like 'Heddlu' and 'milltir' and 'Maes Gwasanaeth Drafford' and you find yourself reading both to try and work out what the Welsh means and, just in time, realise that you have drifted into another lane as a Maserati comes scorching up beside you. What is it all for (answer shortly follows)? Can there, in the history of the internal combustion engine, have been any driver who has breathed a sigh of relief and thought "At last, I can tell where the motorway service area is, now that it's in Welsh"? Could such an improbable figure have driven all the way, say, from Reading, with his bladder bursting, or desperate for a cup of coffee, because he could not understand signs which did not have a Welsh translation?

The answer to the second question is, of course, no. And to the first: it has nothing to do with road safety or information and everything to do with political correctness. I have nothing against Welsh. It sounds very attractive and it is a wholly admirable aim to prevent it from becoming a dead language. There is no question but that it is very good for brain power to have the facility of more than one tongue, and it is wonderful to promote a culture by giving currency to the way that it is expressed through speech; but a touch of reality should occasionally manifest itself. I was in a large supermarket on the edge of Cardiff once and was surprised, no, not really, the better adjective would be 'resigned', to see that all the overhead signs were in two languages. Everything was in English and Welsh, even the blindingly unnecessary *coffee/coffi* and *yoghurt/iogwrt* and even when the word was the same – *salad/salad*. The predicate would, therefore, appear to be that somewhere in Cardiff there are people who speak Welsh but do not understand simple English. In the overwhelmingly unlikely event that they both exist and go shopping in a supermarket, it would be interesting to observe how they get on at the check-out.

This phenomenon is not limited, of course, to Welsh. On the Isle of Man, government departments use letterheads in English and Manx – and the Electricity Authority's and the Water and Sewage Authority's employees drive around in vehicles with the liveries in both languages. The last person who spoke Manx as his native language died nearly forty years ago and he had not been able to chat to another Manx speaker for about ten years before that, so I do not suppose that there is anyone who would not understand who the vans belonged to, if only English appeared on their sides, except, just possibly, for the waiters in the Thai restaurant in Douglas. To be fair, it does no harm and even generates a warm feeling to see that an attempt is being made to revive a moribund language, as long as that is not allowed to override common sense as does, not infrequently, happen, as the following example shows. There was, and for all I know, still is, a judicial post called a Parking Appeals Adjudicator. Although, perhaps, not on a par with the office of Lord Justice of Appeal, it nevertheless had to be held by a qualified lawyer. Note this: in order to be admitted as a solicitor or be called to the Bar, you have to have passed some very intense examinations and they are, of course, in English. It is difficult to imagine, for instance, a barrister presenting his arguments to a High Court judge with much prospect of success if he or she is unable to speak English. The post of principal adjudicator of the Parking Appeals Tribunal was advertised, some years ago, in a number of specialist legal periodicals. The advertisement was inserted by the, then, Lord Chancellor's

Department. It was in English and Welsh. No doubt, the justification for the advertisement's being in two languages was that the successful applicant would be required to sit in Cardiff and Swansea; but it seems to have escaped the notice of the keen logician who made that decision that another condition was that the post also required the holder to sit in Birmingham, Bristol, Manchester, Liverpool, and Leeds. So, had someone managed to qualify as a lawyer without it being noticed that he spoke Welsh but not English, and had he found that it was a bit of a struggle to make a living with that impediment, he would, no doubt have been very grateful to see that there was a job advertisement that he could read and understand (that is, on the assumption that he was able to make out the odd word of English so that he recognised that the journal was intended for legal practitioners), and he would have been even more grateful and, no doubt, surprised, when he was offered (presumably by a bilingual letter) the position as Head of Parking Appeals. The problems would have started when he got to Liverpool for his first tribunal hearing, having overcome the difficulty presented by the absence of Welsh traffic signs in the Merseyside, and found that the proceedings were conducted in English and that the L.C.D. had omitted to provide him with an interpreter.

So, keep the Welsh language thriving, keep Manx and Erse and Cornish alive, resuscitate Anglo-Saxon if you want but, for Heaven's sake use English where it matters. Like on road signs.

BOOK JACKET REVIEWS

Yes, I know that no-one (except, perhaps, the terminally lonely) writes reviews of book jackets, but you realised, surely, that this heading is short-hand for the selective quotations from favourable reviews that you find on paperbacks and the jackets of hardbacks. Who writes them: the author's mother? Time and again you are told that if you read only one book of the genre this year it should be this book. Often you are told that a book is charming or witty or that "I laughed out loud" or that the creator has excelled himself and you buy the book only to give up the struggle to read it before you have finished it, but not before you have searched, in vain, for the "gems of humour", "the lyrical prose" or the "subtle and beautifully observed exploration", all of which is followed by a synopsis which has only a tangential connection with the story that you have striven to get through.

In the unlikely event that this ever gets published, I know that I have given a hostage to fortune here. But, in place of the usual encomia, wouldn't it be more honest to say "One of a surfeit of similar outpourings, from a peppery old fart who can't seem to see the good in anything, who hankers for a dimly-recalled past, and who thinks that he has something original to say". At least, that might make the occasional bookshop browser take a little notice.